*This book is dedicated to the memory of Niall 'Badger' Byrne
—a tireless servant for Monkstown FC and a wonderful friend
who will never be forgotten.*

MUNSTER RUGBY

THE PHENOMENON

To my favourite player;

maverick
house

Published by Maverick House Publishers.

Maverick House, Main Street, Dunshaughlin, Co. Meath, Ireland.
Maverick House SE Asia, 440 Sukhumvit Road, Washington Square, Klongton, Klongtoey,
Bangkok 10110, Thailand.

info@maverickhouse.com
http://www.maverickhouse.com

ISBN: 1-905379-19-6
978-1-905379-19-4

5 4 3 2 1

Printed by Colour Books Ltd.

The paper used in this book comes from the wood pulp of managed forests. For every tree felled at least one tree is planted, thereby renewing natural resources.

A CIP catalogue record for this book is available from the British Library.

Acknowledgements

When writing a book like this you are completely reliant on the generosity of those who answer the phone and agree to contribute. And for that I am eternally grateful. In particular to Mick Galwey, who took time away from coaching the international club side to speak with me. Also George Hook, who along with his own unique opinion, contributed advice and support. A special thank you has to go to Derek Foley, who was always on hand to contribute his expert opinion, no matter when I came calling. Tony Ward is another who deserves a mention, as do Trevor Hogan and Jeremy Staunton. Of course, the biggest thanks must go to the players who never stopped reaching for that rainbow and have given us, the fans, the greatest pleasure of all. To Deirdre, for putting up with me, and to my parents for affording me the opportunity in life to achieve the things I have. To Briain and Joe, whose antics and devotion epitomise everything this book is about, thank you for allowing me tell at least one of your many incredible tales. And to those I have forgotten to mention, I am sorry, but thank you for any help you may have given me, it was all greatly appreciated.

Introduction

Back in 2000, I set off for London with two friends in the hope of seeing Munster lift the Heineken Cup in Twickenham.

Arriving the night before the match, the centre of London may as well have been Patrick Street in Cork or O'Connell Street in Limerick. Everywhere you looked there were intoxicated Paddies, all eager to give another good reason why Munster would win the next day. I joined in the festivities, filled with optimism, a trait we Irish have in abundance (until it is taken over by begrudgery), before marching towards the stadium.

Funnily enough, I don't remember a great deal about the game. I was separated from my two brothers in arms and cast in amongst what could best be described as the prawn sandwich brigade. Amongst the golf claps, whoops and cheers, I began to swallow pints, getting an impending feeling that this was not going to be our day.

I was right; even though Munster scored the only try on the day, they lost. And if there is one thing worse than losing to the English in Twickenham, it's trying to get out of Twickenham. The park itself seems like two train rides, a cab ride, a balloon journey and a pony express away from civilisation.

Of course, when 60,000 people are going in the same direction all at once, things become problematic. Meeting up with my posse, we decided to avoid the rush by camping out in a nearby bar, and began to quaff as many pints as possible whilst dissecting the game.

In the end it was declared a travesty, and all blame was shipped upon referee Joel Dumé of France. The only way to appease this terrible feeling of pain, loss and misery was with more pints, more festivities, and some reckless behaviour around Soho. We were not alone. Indeed, it seemed like most of Munster had the same idea.

Throngs of middle-aged men and women mixed with lads and girls barely out of their teens, respectable businessmen sang songs in the middle of the streets, their red Munster jerseys barely holding in their stomachs, and people from every corner of the province joined in the revelry that could have been so much more joyous had Munster actually won. Loans and overdrafts were momentarily forgotten. The prospect of returning home with no money didn't matter; all that mattered was being there for Munster—for the team and for the fans, gathered together on foreign soil once more.

On many occasions I have been asked what it is that appeals to a bunch of grown men, and in some cases women, that propels them to tog out in less than flattering garments and knock lumps out of each other in some of the worst weather conditions known to man. But the same question applies to each fan: what is it that makes you save up for six months, abstaining from beer, food and that Sting concert you have always wanted to go to, only to blow the lot, for example, in a dank Irish bar in some corner of France in two bleary nights?

The answer simply lies in the power and allure of the game of rugby, and in particular the romantic attraction that is encompassed by the Munster Rugby team.

I am one of the many disciples of Webb Ellis who has spent almost four days a week training and playing for the glory of club and occasionally province, over nearly 18 years.

Through hell, high water and even driving snow, I have waded on a waterlogged pitch in a desperate attempt to get some form of one-upmanship on some opponent who is in exactly the same boat as me.

But as unappealing as this may seam to the casual reader, this is what I live for, and in the immortal words of Joni Mitchell, 'You don't know what you got 'til it's gone'. And that is the true secret to the code of Rugby Union; once you are bitten by the bug it is absolutely impossible to quit.

Take the team that I am dutifully bound to, Monkstown FC, in the epicentre of Dublin's metropolitan rugby playing teams, and a mere dart stop from IRFU headquarters at Lansdowne Road. If rugby is perceived to be a snotty 'West Brit' sport that only the likes of Ross O'Carroll-Kelly play, then this area is the reason.

The pitches of these 'old boy' clubs alone are worth millions, and by God do they know it. I would be lying if I did not add that the air of pseudo-elitism that emanates from many of these ports in a D4 rugby storm can prevent many an independent punter from ever returning.

But in truth it is a façade, an itch that may never be scratched, and has been inherited from years of simply being at the top of the game. And in the end what may seem like blatant bravado is little more than a ruse designed to attract the better players from other provinces, in a desperate attempt to cling on to the past.

The once respected old boy networks, where elitist men played for their country, are now facing country opposition. People who would once upon a time never have been allowed set foot through the front gates are now beating them. Times have changed, and at Monkstown there are more country players on the first team than Dubs. This is a trend mirrored throughout the suburbs.

The introduction of these country members has changed the internal spirit of all clubs, and much like enlargement in the EU, we are all the better for it. Our Euro is our love for the game, and it is a currency that is taken in every club in Ireland, not just the elite, premier All Ireland League clubs. It transcends age, sex and experience, and has become the new poster boy for provincial and international teams.

Earlier this year, after a rigorous training session, I quickly escaped from my muddy gear and tip-toed through the pools of brown, mucky water into the communal showers. Straight away, I was presented with the wonderful sight of Pajo, a naked 50-something year old prop, showering beside his 19 year old son. Both were playing on the same team, and in the secret veil of a steamy shower were discussing some form of Machiavellian strategy to use in the next game.

Where the man got his nickname I don't think anyone knows, but what we do know is that he epitomises the new spirit of modern rugby. He is a diamond in the rough, his never-say-never attitude summing up the spirit that has vaulted rugby in Ireland to its most popular status in a century, and Munster Rugby to the fore of the modern game.

And with all due respect to Leinster Rugby, with whom I now ply my trade and have been capped by their junior representative side, I believe we all have a lot to learn from our southern brethren. In my experience, there is something lurking in Munster Rugby that simply does not exist within the other provinces.

Be it the sixth sense that only blesses the super heroes, or a simple God-given understanding of the sacred game that may as well be in French for the rest of us mortal fools, this in-built extra something is an edge that is present in the provincial club that boasts the home of Irish rugby, who have now, finally, after years of heartbreak, been crowned the European champions.

My first experience with the phenomenon that is Munster Rugby came at the tender age of 18, when I was selected to play for the Connaught Youths team. In our first game against Ulster in the Sportsground in Galway city, we dispatched a fairly lacklustre side. With that win under the belt, spirits in the Con camp were fairly high, as the next week we set off down to Highfield in Cork for the game against Munster.

The day of the game we talked about the Munster team and their strengths and weaknesses. In particular, I have a clear recollection of deciding on how to cope with their star number eight, who at the time was known as Big Donnacha (can you guess who that is?). There was also some prattle about two Cronin brothers who were destined for great things: the usual pre-match banter. And in spite of all our talk, preparation and Guy Fawkes-like planning, we were beaten; badly.

In the first five minutes, the Munster prop ran all of 20 metres up the touchline, past a winger, and scored a try. Where he came from I'll never know, but he wasn't on the list of stars that we had prepared and watched out for. And that day I realised something valuable about Munster—there are no key players, no pariahs and no prima donnas in the Munster set-up: the prop is as likely to stick the nail in your coffin as the full back, and you underestimate them at your peril.

The next day, the headline on the match report in the Cork Examiner read: 'Mighty Munster overturn cocky Connaught'. The harsh world of the media opened a proverbial can of whoopass on our performance, even though we had only lost by ten points.

Some ten years later I once again took to the field of battle to face Munster, this time togging out for the Leinster Juniors. I remember trotting out on to the pitch with a wry smile on my face thinking, 'This time I will have revenge.' I was even coming up with some catchy headlines of my own to post down to the *Examiner*.

Once again I was to learn a lesson from the men of Munster. On paper we were man for man better than them, but during the game they were quite simply a better team. We wanted to win but they knew they would. How the hell do you get that divine sense of self belief, that X-factor? Whatever it is, it only seems to work for them.

Yet despite being from Galway and having taken many a good beating from the southern men, there is something about them that has made me their number one fan. A feeling that clouded all my wits and gut feelings and led me astray to the depths of Soho that fateful Cup final day it may be, but a powerful feeling it is none the less. And with time against me and slowly running out of provinces to play for, I have decided to try and find out what it is that makes Munster at all levels a winning province. Certainly that X-factor is as obvious as the beating doled out by the Munster men this year to the Sale Sharks at Thomond.

It is a concept, an ideal, wrapped in a red enigma that only comes out during a full moon in Limerick at a Heineken Cup game. Certainly it is a fragile ingredient that can melt away at crucial, pivotal moments of the most important matches, just as easily as it roars into life, pummelling the favourites and snatching victory from the jaws of defeat.

For those that have never made it to the hallowed ground of Thomond, it is a feeling that cannot be described with words, but is simply a chorus of 30,000 raucous fans, joining together to form that extra man, that overlap, or that unnerving chant. Yet away from home that *Je ne sais quoi* can also be as powerful, which once again adds to the strangeness of the phenomenon.

What this variable is I do not know, but over the course of this book I will try to discover and name it, or more importantly, get those who are closest to it to try and explain.

***

The best place to start is at the beginning, and in order to fully understand the draw, the appeal, the very essence of what it is to be a rugby fan, and from there a Munster Rugby fan, a short history of the game itself is required.

At some point or other in life a rugby player has found him or herself standing out on the wing while ice cold, driving rain is pelting down from the heavens. The opposition is so good that the only chance you have of touching the ball is when they kick the conversion. Your jersey is now a clammy, icy drape that has doubled in weight, and every time it brushes against your skin the chaffing increases.

The one pertinent question that hits you in a rare moment of epiphany is ... why? Why would anybody in their right mind concede to play this ridiculous sport? I mean, what sort of a sadist concocts a game that is basically designed to encourage physical aggression?

Once again, the answer lies across the water, from our colonial donors in the form of the Queen's England. Much like the potato and the Customs House, rugby is an import from the Brits.

Not surprisingly, rugby descended from the British upper classes, who passed it on to our fair country, and the story of its conception is part of legend, even inscribed on the World Cup trophy itself. The legendary story about the origin of Rugby football, whereby a young man named William Webb Ellis 'took the ball in his arms (i.e. caught the ball) and ran' while playing football at Rugby School in England is now in the lore of Rugby history.

However, some sports historians have dismissed the story as unlikely since an official investigation by the Old Rugbeian Society in 1895. But in true rugby fashion, the governing body of the RFU prefer the romantic notion of a legendary conception and have christened the trophy for the Rugby Union World Cup as the 'Webb Ellis', in his honour, and a plaque at the school 'commemorates' the 'achievement'.

While the game undoubtedly did start in England's public schools, these bastardised football games had probably taken place at Rugby School for 200 years before someone had the bright idea of writing a description of the game down and patenting it. In fact, much like many a junior match in the depths of winter in Ireland today, until the formation of the Football Association (FA) in October 1863, each team would be forced to agree on a set of rules with opponents before a match.

Teams competing against each other regularly would tend to agree to play a similar style of football, (something like the chaps in Dublin 4 playing against the other chaps in Anglesea Road).

Rugby football has a claim to the world's first 'football club', formed as Guy's Hospital Football Club, London, in 1843, by Rugby School old boys. A number of other clubs formed to play games based on the Rugby School rules and it was not long before the game took to the boats and came to Ireland to find a new home of its own.

First stop was the beautiful grounds of the Dublin University Football Club (Trinity College) pavilions. And, being the world's oldest surviving rugby football club, having been formed in 1854, Trinity has led the way for the game in the Emerald Isle, currently still playing rugby in the All Ireland League Division One.

Four years later, back in England the game continued to develop and Blackheath Rugby Club was founded in 1858 and is the oldest continuously-existing rugby club in England.

It was also a founding member of The Football Association.

When it became clear that the FA would not agree to rules which allowed 'hacking' and 'hacking over' (fundamental parts of the rugby game), Blackheath withdrew from the FA just over a month after the initial meeting. Other rugby clubs followed this lead and did not join the FA.

For the next few years, rugby clubs continued to agree rules before the start of each game as they had always done, but on January 26, 1871, the Rugby Football Union (RFU) formed, leading to the standardisation of the rules for all clubs in England that played a variety of the Rugby School laws. Soon, most countries with a sizable rugby community had formed their own national unions.

Ireland was no exception to this, and despite all the happenings in the country, and in full accordance with the ongoing GAA ban, the game flourished. In 1886, the International Rugby Board (IRB) became the world governing and law-making body for rugby. The RFU recognised it as such in 1890.

By now the game had spread to the Southern Hemisphere and one country who would later define the sport took to the oval ball.

The introduction of Rugby Football Union into New Zealand was by Charles John Monro, son of Sir David Monro, who was then speaker of the New Zealand House of Representatives.

The younger Monro had been sent to Christ's College, East Finchley in North London, England. That school had adopted rugby rules and Monro became an enthusiastic convert. He brought the game back to his native Nelson, and arranged the first rugby match between Nelson College and Nelson Football Club on May 14, 1870. The rest is history, and the Kiwis took to the pitch like ducks to water, eventually developing it into their national sport.

Today they are the strongest nation in the world when it comes to Rugby Union, a fact mirrored by the statistic that only one Irish team has ever beaten them—Munster. To this date the Irish national side has never managed to topple the All Blacks.

Of course, throughout Rugby's development, it was always played by the upper classes. 'A thugs game played by gentlemen', was the popular moniker. England's working class towns saw fit to change this, and in the 1890s a clash of cultures erupted into a revolution between the working men's rugby clubs of northern England and the southern clubs of gentlemen. It was a dispute revolving around money and the nature of professionalism within the game.

On 29 August, 1895, clubs split from the RFU and met at the George Hotel in Huddersfield to form the Northern Rugby Football Union, commonly called the Northern Union. NRFU rules gradually diverged from those of rugby union, although the name Rugby League did not become official until the Northern Rugby League formed in 1901. The name Rugby Football League dates from 1922.

A similar split occurred in Australia and other rugby playing nations in the Southern Hemisphere. Initially, rugby league in Australia operated under the same rules as rugby union. But after a tour of Australia and Great Britain by a professional New Zealand team in 1907, and an Australian Rugby League tour of Great Britain the next year; rugby league teams in the Southern Hemisphere adopted rugby league rules.

For clarity and convenience it became necessary to differentiate between the two codes of rugby. The code played by those teams who remained in national organisations which were members of the IRB became known as Rugby Union. The code played by those teams which played 'open' rugby and allowed professionals became known as Rugby League.

Although the IRB claimed to be enforcing the amateur status of rugby union, many referred to the situation as 'shamateurism'. On 26 August, 1995, the IRB declared Rugby Union an 'open' game and removed all restrictions on payments or benefits to those connected with the game. The move from amateurism to professionalism has been one of great success and has undoubtedly increased the quality of rugby being played. However, professionalism has meant a huge increase in the gap between the top nations and the second tier.

Alongside the success stories there have been some famous rugby clubs which have not coped well with the new era. A microcosm of this occurred in Ireland. When the game went professional, many of the four tiers in the All Ireland League (AIL) began forking out wads of cash in order to import the best players from all the ends of the earth. But at the same, the provincial teams were also recruiting the top players to play in maverick new competitions like the Heineken Cup.

As a result, clubs found they had shelled out wads of cash for top players only to find them turning out for their province instead of their home teams. Many clubs felt the pinch for this and found themselves slipping back into a forced case of amateurism. As a result, the quality of the AIL diminished and the attendance figures suffered greatly. In turn this affected the revenue of the top clubs and the League once again suffered as a result. As the provincial game got stronger and stronger, the AIL was forced to play a secondary role to the provincial structure.

At present the AIL structure is under review by the IRFU but appears to have finally found its place in the Irish rugby hierarchy. This year showed signs of rejuvenation within the grass roots structure and the emergence of a club international side that played at Lansdowne Road. Despite this rebirth, there was a clear winner within the new professional era; provincial rugby.

And one team would emerge as the kings of Ireland and the European game; Munster.

MUNSTER RUGBY FACT:

Why fair play pays

When banned in 1996 for some unsightly behaviour on the pitch, Peter 'The Claw' Clohessy lost his professional rugby contract, costing him IR£20,000. He said afterwards: 'Do you know I lost my contract, and that ban in 1996 cost me 20 grand?'

'I suppose at the time I did have a problem over discipline, but when it started costing me money, I had a chat with myself.'

'This is great for Munster and the whole country.'
– Donnacha O'Callaghan

Chapter 1: The IRFU bridging North and South

Lansdowne Road is the undisputed heart of Irish rugby. It is the oldest rugby stadium in the world, steeped in history, but strangely situated in the middle of Dublin's affluent suburbs. On match days, these usually quiet streets are filled with excitement and tension, and an atmosphere of reverence. It is where every player wants to be, the reward for making it through the system and becoming one of the best.

My own first trip to the hallowed turf in Dublin 4 was in 1995, when myself and four friends had come to see Ireland play Scotland. The dart station runs at the back of the South Terrace, and if you can manage to beat the crowd, allows for a speedy getaway from the grounds after the match. Wait just a few minutes though, and you will find yourself in the middle of a crowd of thousands, queuing for over an hour to be transported back towards the city centre.

The man at the dart station offered us his advice on getting out early.

'It just gets so packed bud, you won't get on one for at least an hour,' he said in a raspy Dublin accent. With a 2.30pm kick off, we were desperately hoping to make the 6pm train back to Galway, and were hoping this sage-like Dubliner would give us the inside information needed to make the cunning get away.

'What time should I leave then?' I asked.

'I'll tell you, go into the ground now, get a good spot, and when the ground is full and the teams run out on the pitch, you should leave, bud. That's about the only way to beat the crowd—bleedin' culchies.'

Then he laughed his way down the platform, leaving us confused, angry and a little scared.

Still, we went to the game, Ireland won, and the strangest thing happened. We couldn't leave the ground. Pitch invasions were commonplace back then and once we managed to get on to the pitch, we didn't want to leave it.

Even the thoughts of hanging around the less than attractive halls of the bus depot with the down and outs and junkies couldn't make us leave the turf. We stayed there for as long as we could until we were eventually chucked out by the stewards who told us, 'It's managed to stay intact for over 100 years and you're not going to ruin it now'.

As it turns out now we could have done all the damage we wanted to, as Lansdowne is soon to be subject to a controversial new makeover by the IRFU and the FAI. The new grounds will constitute an end of days for the back pitches of Lansdowne as the pitch is moved around to allow for an all-encompassing 60,000-seater stadium.

And while this is happening, Brian O'Driscoll will pack his bags and with the rest of the national squad trundle off to the north side, to play in the incredible Croke Park, home of a very different game. Despite all kinds of rumours, whispering that Lansdowne will never receive its facelift once rugby and soccer gain a firm foothold in Croker, the IRFU maintains it will keep its head office and grounds at Lansdowne Road.

In addition, the Union also owns Ravenhill Park in Belfast, Thomond Park in Limerick, and a number of grounds in provincial areas that have been rented to clubs. And the sacred confines of Limerick's Thomond is also due to get a daub of rouge and a dabble of concrete in a project that will increase the capacity to over 25,000.

While these two proposed developments have eaten up many columns of newspaper ink, historically the IRFU always put stock in its property and grounds, and looking back at the origins of the rugby set-up in Ireland, there has always been huge geographical importance placed on the game, something that may well be a contributing factor in the Munster phenomenon. This seems obvious now when we look at the support and celebration that accompanied Munster to glory in Cardiff, but it had its origins in the very formation of the game's structure in this country.

Initially, there were two unions, both founded in 1874. The Irish Football Union had jurisdiction over clubs in Leinster, Munster and parts of Ulster; the Northern Football Union of Ireland controlled the Belfast area. The IRFU was formed in 1879 as an amalgamation of the two different organisations, and branches were formed in Leinster, Munster and Ulster.

And almost like the poor adopted son of the west, the Connaught Branch was founded in 1886 (although some argue it only was taken seriously when Michael Bradley became coach).

Of course the fierce political makeup of the island had a dramatic influence on the sport and as the north/south divide grew, the Committee of the Irish Rugby Football Union decided that it would continue to administer its affairs on the basis of the 32

Irish counties and the traditional four provinces of Ireland—Connaught, Leinster, Munster and Ulster.

This was a unique sporting outlook that was maverick and revolutionary at the time and managed to make the game a 32 county sport—something that soccer was unable to do.

Of course it meant that the Irish representative teams were drawn from players from two separate political territories: the Republic of Ireland, and Northern Ireland, still part of the United Kingdom. Still, the game managed to transcend the sectarian boundaries that stayed very much erect over the past 90 years.

In an effort to sustain the unity of Irish rugby union and to reinforce the bonds built between North and South, the IRFU purchased a new ground in 1923 in the Ravenhill district of Belfast, at a cost of £2,300.

While the last full international at Ravenhill took place in the 1953-54 season against Scotland—who were victorious by 2 tries (6 points) to nil—it has become a fortress for the Ulster White Knights, who until 2006 had remained the only Irish side to lift the Heineken Cup.

One of the main reasons cited by the IRFU for the success of this cross-boundary support was that players in the North and South shared a similar outlook and background—educated at private boarding schools and generally unionist in outlook—even if they differed in religion. And even though the sport has diversified and reached the four corners of the country, that situation is similar today.

The strongholds of Irish rugby in the south, outside of Munster, remain the Ivy League fee-paying private schools, evident in the Leinster Schools Cup competition. The same can be said up north, where the majority of rugby clubs and players are of Protestant religion, with one red hand reaching across the water, striking allegiance with England. Yet both North and South have managed to co-exist quite happily for almost a century.

Of course, things didn't always run as smoothly as the IRFU would have liked. In recent years, controversy raged over the issue of anthems being attributed with the national side. In the past, when Irish internationals were played alternatively in Belfast and Dublin, 'God Save the Queen' was played up north while 'Amhrán na bhFiann' was sung in Dublin. Of course as games ceased to be played in Ravenhill, so ended the tradition of 'God Save the Queen'. Yet for many of the Irish internationals like David Humphreys, the Irish national anthem was not his. After much debate, 'Amhrán na bhFiann' has been replaced in away games by 'Ireland's Call', a 32 county song for the Irish rugby side, penned by Phil Coulter.

On a domestic level, this cross border consideration continued as teams from the North and South played regularly in cup competitions. During the 1880s, the four provincial branches of the IRFU first ran cup competitions and these tournaments still take place every year.

However, with the foundation of the All Ireland League in 1990 the significance of the cup competition has been diminished. The AIL comprises 50 senior clubs from the 32 counties who fight it out in a fiercely competitive format to become All Ireland Champions each year. Since the advent of the professional era, the AIL has come under direct criticism from critics who believe that the competition is dead, with all good players signing for the provinces.

The four provinces have played an Interprovincial Championship since the 1920s and continue to be the focal point for players aspiring to the international level. Munster, Leinster and Ulster continue to be the strongest three and have made inroads in the highest rugby competition in the Northern Hemisphere: the Heineken Cup. Connaught in the west of the country has continued to grow and impress in the European Plate competition.

There are presently around 60,000 players in total in Ireland.

* 56 clubs are affiliated to the Ulster Branch.
* 71 to the Leinster Branch.
* 59 to the Munster Branch.
* 19 to the Connaught Branch.

In addition, there are 246 Schools playing rugby; Ulster (107), Leinster (75), Munster (41) and Connaught (23).

***

But as my friends and I were being chased from the sacred walls of Lansdowne Road that day, we began shouting up at the IRFU crest that sits above one of the stadium gates. 'We'll be back and next time we will be playing,' screamed one of my mates.

The history that seeps through the terraces and walls of the ground is inspirational and we took that feel good factor back to Loughrea and that year reached the Under 16 Connaught League final, the first underage Loughrea team to do that.

We left in good spirits, inspired to make it back as players, and in the end only had to wait a few minutes for a dart, the majority of the crowd having dispersed while we were running around the pitch for an hour. We had missed the train, but standing on the main pitch at Lansdowne Road would more than make up for that.

Anybody who is even slightly interested in Irish rugby will understand the significance, the effect the atmosphere has on the fans, the players, everyone involved.

I have since played twice on the main pitch at Lansdowne Road, fulfilling a dream, yet that hour had more of an impression on me than any game played there could ever have, and to this day I am glad we missed the train.

Nobody beats Munster twice, not in the Heineken Cup, and I'll stand by that. It is an incredible competition.'
– Mick Galwey

Chapter 2: The Heineken Cup

The Heineken Cup was a huge factor in propelling provincial rugby in Ireland on to centre stage, and ensured an unrivalled support for its teams; particularly Munster. It began in 1995-96 with a dozen sides representing Ireland, Wales, Italy, Romania and France. Much like a test run for the main event, and almost a template for the later Celtic League, the competition was later refined into the finished product on display today.

The Romanian teams soon dropped out, and although no definitive reason for this was given, the financial strain of competing all over Europe was considered by many as the straw that broke the camel's back. Also missing that first year were the English and Scottish teams who refrained from competition until 1996-97, as they were already committed to their domestic schedules.

From an inauspicious beginning in Romania, where Toulouse thrashed Farul Constanta 54-10 in front of a small crowd, the competition gathered momentum and crowds grew. While Toulouse went on to become the first European Rugby Champions, eventually beating the world renowned Cardiff RFC in extra time, something bigger was brewing in a province a mere two-day ferry journey away.

French giants Brive won the next tournament, led by the inspired Christoph Lamaison, and reached the final again in 1997-98 where they were beaten late in the game by Bath and a Jonathan Callard penalty kick.

This victory by the Bath faithful should have kick-started the English clubs into a European frenzy. However, instead they decided to withdraw from the competition altogether due to a dispute between European Rugby and the RFU over fixture scheduling and money.

Without English clubs, the 1998-99 tournament revolved around the Celtic fringes, France and Italy. For the fourth consecutive year, a French club, in the shape of Colomiers from the Toulouse suburbs, reached the final. But it was Ulster, playing at Lansdowne Road, who carried home the trophy after a 21-6 win. David Humphreys and his White Knights descended on Lansdowne Road that year and against all the odds (but to be fair no English) they conquered the touring French.

Before this season, they remained the only Irish team to have lifted the European Rugby Cup, although they have never really featured outside of the group stages since, (and it didn't really look like that was going to change this year unless O'Driscoll's Leinster men could do something about it.) Obviously seeing what they were missing, the next year would see the return of the English clubs.

The competition had changed slightly and the pool stages were spread over three months to allow the competition to develop alongside the nations' own domestic competitions, and the knockout stages were scheduled to take the tournament into the early spring.

Much like the Champions League in football, the top five teams from France and England would gain automatic access to the competition. Four from Wales' domestic championship would secure entry along with the top three provinces in Ireland. Both Scotland and Italy were designated two automatic places. The remaining four places in the 24 team tournament are allocated on a meritocracy basis. The rules of the competition set down by the ERC are as follows:

- No country can earn more than one meritocracy place and the extra places are based on performance by the clubs from each country.

- Nations who have a team that reaches the semi-finals are guaranteed an extra place the following season. If a country has more than one team in the semi-finals, then the criteria is based on quarter-final places and then Pool results.

- Each nation sets its own criteria for qualification for the Heineken Cup. Clubs that do not qualify for the Heineken Cup can enter the European Rugby Shield.

- Six pools of four teams play both home and away games. Four points are awarded for a win and two points for a draw.

- Much Like the Super 14 competition in the Southern Hemisphere, a bonus point is awarded for a loss by seven points or fewer, or for scoring four tries or more.

The 1999-2000 competition was decided with a final between Munster and Northampton, with Northampton coming out on top by a single point. Though they fell at the last hurdle, this was the year when Munster Rugby would emerge as arguably the saviours of the European competition. They brought romance and excitement back to the competition.

Tradition stated that home support was an almost unbeatable factor, with partisan home crowds allowing for a good thrashing, but one team was bucking the trend, following their heroes in red, turning away stadiums into the River Styx, surrounded by a bellowing of vocal support.

This fanatical devotion that was devoid of all but a few clubs was to gather momentum over the year as Munster banked and weaved on the hunt for European glory. The chase would generate more column inches in the press, both home and abroad, than the national team could ever hope to do.

Through an incredible campaign, driven from the impenetrable fortress of Thomond Park, Munster waged war on a competition that was to become their Tower of Babel. And after beating Stade Français and the seemingly unconquerable Toulouse, it seemed that year had to be Munster's.

Captain Mick Galwey dedicated the final to the legions of travelling support that had left the team 'speechless', during the quarter and semi-finals.

'We want to win this for all the right reasons,' he said. 'For Munster, their marvellous supporters, for ourselves, and, we believe, for everyone in Ireland. Winning the European Cup is the ultimate aim, and that's why we are here. That's why we intend to bring the European Cup through Shannon Airport's customs to the delight of our supporters.'

Yet through a series of near misses and poor fortune Munster were found wanting and Northampton sneaked a famous victory—leaving Galwey with one promise that he couldn't keep.

This final would serve a double blow to the Irish faithful as talismanic hooker Keith Wood would depart the following season for London club Harlequins.

In an emotional interview before the final, Wood attempted to describe what it was that made this Munster phenomenon work:

'There are players here that you have grown up with, in the same city or town or village, met at schools or at under age level, played with at your club, and you have been aware of them all the time. I've been amazed and pleased this time round with the Munster set up and it has really settled us into a cohesive unit. In the end though, it will all come down to the game, it's just a game and the team that plays better on the day will win. I just want to win.'

Woody did not get the dream send-off he was looking for and the mighty men from the south of Ireland were vanquished by Northampton. But despite the result, Munster, through its fanatical supporters, had shown the whole of European rugby a statement of intent—we will be back.

Since then the tournament has gone from strength to strength, with Leicester Tigers becoming the first side to successfully defend their title, beating Stade Français in 2001.

The next year saw the Munster men return to centre stage, and the final. Galwey and his charges were propelled to the final in the Millennium Stadium against the reigning champions Leicester, led by the imposing figure of Martin Johnson.

Yet once again the rugby gods turned their back on the Munster men who turned an 80,000 seater stadium into their own private supporters group. That Saturday it must have been very lonely indeed around the fields of Athenry; the banks were breached and everyone had gone east from Garryowen as a red army of supporters invaded Cardiff.

But on the world's stage, rugby would take second place as the Tiger's flanker Neil Back produced a piece of larceny that Ronnie Biggs would have been proud of, illegally knocking the ball out of Peter Stringer's paws as Munster were laying siege to the Leicester line. The ball was dropped. The scoring chance was gone. The dream was over.

The end result would break thousands of hearts as the silver chalice was once again ripped away from the hands of the deserving and placed back in the cabinet of the Tigers.

Life has not gotten any easier for Munster as they knocked repeatedly on the door of glory, only to have it shut in their face time and time again. In 2002/2003, they reached the quarter-finals after an unbelievable, fairytale win against Gloucester, later issued on DVD under the title 'The Miracle Match'. In this game, Munster needed to win by a margin of at least 27 points and score a minimum of four tries. They won 33-6, with four tries in a game that has become part of Munster rugby folklore.

They faced Leicester at Welford Road and defeated the reigning champions to progress to the semi-finals. They faced Toulouse in the semi-finals, but lost out on a place in the final after losing by a single point in France. Munster hearts were broken again, and the red army of fans could only watch and think of what might have been as Toulouse's victory over French rivals Perpignan meant that they joined the Tigers as the only team to win the title twice.

The 2004 competition was just as painful, and saw English side London Wasps defeat Munster in Lansdowne Road in one of the most thrilling semi-finals ever. They went on to beat Toulouse at Twickenham to win the Heineken Cup for the first time, leaving Munster again dwelling on what might have been.

In the 2005 final, Toulouse became the first club to win the title three times, defeating another French club, Stade Français of Paris, at Murrayfield.

2006 saw this glorious competition go from strength to strength, producing some of the most thrilling games of rugby football ever to grace Europe's sporting pantheon. And of course, once again, the impossible was made look easy as Thomond Park, Limerick repelled the invaders of Zurich Premiership giants Sale Sharks in a thrilling performance. Needing to win by four tries, and secure a bonus point, Munster (with more than a little help from their home supporters) devoured Jason Robinson and his charges.

From there, well, we all know what happened next …

Due to thrilling matches like these and the sheer spirit and determination on view week in, week out, the roller coaster competition has not escaped the attention of the media moguls and Sky Sports (under the watchful eyes of Rupert Murdoch) have secured the rights to the cherished competition.

From now on Irish punters will have to forgo the witty banter and vitriolic analysis of George Hook and Brent Pope and instead face the limp and partisan drivel of Dewi Morris and Stuart Barnes. The competition has generated wads of cash for television stations, advertising agents, pubs, clubs and touts, but has also elevated the game to another level. And it is on this European stage that one little corner of Europe, one quarter of an island, has managed to captivate the world.

Fuelled by passion, pride and a little *Je ne sais quoi*, the men from Munster have made the Champion's League of Rugby and turned it into their own fairytale.

What it is that has driven them year after year in search of the happy ending they have finally reached is hopefully contained in the following pages.

MUNSTER RUGBY FACT:

The Referee in the Final

Chris White, who refereed the 2006 final in the Millennium Stadium in Cardiff, created Heineken Cup history by becoming the first man to preside over three Heineken Cup finals. As well as officiating over Munster's incredible win, the 42 year old former junior school teacher from Cheltenham also controlled the Toulouse versus Perpignan final in 2003 and the other all-French affair last year between Toulouse and Stade Français in Edinburgh.

'Leinster, to be fair, are playing lovely rugby at the moment, but there is something about Munster and the Heineken Cup that is special. I mean their record is great. Okay, they haven't won it, even though they have twice been to the final, but their record on the road in France, Leicester, Gloucester—there are so many that have contributed to this amazing journey and yet it hasn't reached its destination yet.

'I really believe that it is fantastic, and I believe that it is part of the appeal that Munster still hasn't got there but they are still chasing it, and the media are chasing it, and the fans.

'I go to all the Leinster school games here in Donnybrook, and the amount of people that you see wearing their Munster colours is just unbelievable, and they have no connection whatsoever with the province. They are Leinster people, and they go away with Munster people and they support them both at home and away and that is something you only get with Munster and is something that started off back when we beat the All Blacks.'

But did players keep building themselves up again and again after facing the most gut-wrenching and cruel defeats, snatched from the jaws of victory? What is it about that red jersey that seems to give the players the strength and courage to do it?

'I'll tell you what it is about Munster that makes them different to all the other teams in the competition. The ultimate aim for every sportsman is to play for your country, whatever the sport, but I can honestly say with my hand on my heart that even in my time, when you put on the Munster jersey, particularly in Limerick, there was something special about it.

'And I can say that with an insight because I played the last two years of representative rugby for Leinster and there was no comparison. With Leinster, playing in those days was a means to an end. You played for Leinster with a view to stepping up to the national side, but you played for Munster to win at all costs, and that was the end in itself. If the step up to international rugby followed, then so be it, but at the time the pride in the jersey was all that mattered.

'There was no ulterior motive other than playing for the province and it is the same today as it was then, just like when we beat the All Blacks, and I think that is unique and uniquely Munster. For me that is why they are special.

Of course, there were down sides when you played with your club in Limerick. Such was the passion of the fans that if you were on the opposing team, then nothing was sacred. Anybody you knew, cared about or loved was subjected to a high level of abuse. That was, of course, until you put on the crimson pullover with the Munster crest on it. And of course Ward played for one of those teams.

'When I played for Garryowen everybody hated them. We were like the Manchester United of rugby because we were the successful side and everyone that went to Limerick tended to be attracted by Garryowen. They simply had the network to bring people in and get them a job or whatever.

'When I played against Young Munster's or Shannon or Crescent or Bohemians I was hated by their fans. I mean, the abuse you used to take from the fans was like something you would see the guys in the Premiership get these days, some really vile things.

'But when you went out and played in a Munster shirt on a Saturday in Thomond Park and the same people—because you knew the faces—were there on the sideline cheering you on and screaming at every good thing you did, it was just unbelievable.

'The tables were turned and you went from the scum of the earth to the king of the world, and that really was a great feeling, until the next club game anyway. And that added to that special pride you only got from playing for Munster.'

Ward's words made it clear that it meant something special to be a part of Munster, and that maybe this feeling and sense of provincial pride is what keeps the red army moving, consistently defying the odds in the quest to achieve greatness. The message was starting to sink in, but by now the stands were beginning to fill, and as both sets of fans began to chant at each other it was time to part. Ward had to get on with his job and I had to try and get the feeling back into my hands and feet.

MUNSTER RUGBY FACT:

What happens when a
Heineken Cup final is drawn?

People often wonder what would happen if a final was tied at the end of normal play, as this has never actually come to pass. Contrary to popular belief, there would not be a penalty shoot-out. The procedure is as follows:

a) Extra time of 30 minutes (15 per half) will try to decide the tie.

b) If at the end of extra time both teams are still locked, then it is the team who has scored most tries in the final that will lift the trophy.

c) If both teams have scored the same amount of tries in the final, then it is the team that has scored most tries in the quarter and semi-finals who is declared the winner.

 d) After that, if the teams are still level, it goes down to the team that has scored the most points combined in the quarters, semi, and final.

e) If after all that the teams are still deadlocked, the title is shared.

'It's a known fact that Munster people don't go on holidays anymore, they go to Munster matches.'
– Mick Galwey

Chapter 4: Key players and where they came from

Traditionally the game of rugby has been played by the white collar brigade, starting from the halls and pitches of the Ivy-league schools in Leinster and Ulster.

As a result, coverage of the game was always restricted to the broadsheet media, finding a home in the sports pages in *The Irish Times* and the *Irish Independent*. Over decades, columnists like Ned Van Esbeck and later Gerry Thornley became the middlemen for those interested in following the international and provincial progress on a regular basis.

However, the phenomenal growth of Munster Rugby, along with the success of Limerick and Cork teams in the AIL, was to change all this. The prolific support of teams like Shannon and Cork Constitution created a market in the Irish red tops for the game of rugby, the overwhelming demand leading to rugby grabbing a regular spot in the Irish tabloids.

One paper to seize the opportunity was the *Irish Daily Star* and its regular rugby correspondent Derek Foley. From the off, Foley and the *Star* realised the potential that lay within Munster, and they began with extensive coverage of the province's domestic teams.

As a direct result Foley was there when the Heineken Cup journey began, and has extensive knowledge of both the provincial and club set-up within Munster. During the Heineken Cup, his devotion to covering the good, the bad and the downright upsetting of the Munster journey has made him one of the most read, and readable, rugby journalists on the circuit.

Foley categorically believes that another of the components that makes the phenomenon of Munster work is the club set up and their participation in the All Ireland League.

'What happened with the team was indigenous to the geography of the province. They owned something that was a secret and it was involved with the community down there, and then it spread out almost miraculously to the ex-pats and exiles of Munster.

'Declan Kidney likes to tell the story of when he took charge of his first match. It was a Wednesday afternoon and people and players had to get time off work and there was nobody there, maybe 20 people. Now that game has become like the 1916 Rising, with everybody coming up to him claiming they were there when the whole campaign started.

'What happened was that word of mouth began to spread, and who knows, maybe the Young Munster club wanted to be pally with Garryowen, but they couldn't. The Cork and Limerick teams had a rivalry in the past that had been cut throat. In fact, the team selection for Munster is still driven down the middle and the politics of where they play the matches is still a factor.

'Yet the supporters who were essentially from these dividing clubs began to find something in common and the next thing you had Young Munster's passion mixing with Cork Constitution's passion. Even North Kerry and that forgotten county of Tipperary had a chance to get in amongst the sacred mix. And Tipperary was an unusual county, as even though it had that highly regarded club of Clanwilliam, it was always left out of the mix—yet this rolling Munster band wagon picked it up on the road to success.'

One of the things that has been really noticeable is that if you were to pick a team of 15 Tipperary players ten years ago, maybe one or two of them would be recognisable. But to do that now you could pick a Tipp team that would represent that county and do very well. At the route of this growth of rugby in the southern counties was the All Ireland League.

'When the AIL started out it was everything. The other day I was reading a quote from the legendary Sean Diffney in the *Rothman's Rugby Yearbook* that he had written in the second year of the AIL, and he was asking whether the AIL was set up as some sort of Limerick subsidiary and if it was healthy for the game as a whole. In truth, he hit a *zeitgeist* and said, 'Look, this is what is happening, and at the time the AIL was a tremendous feeder for Munster, and you have got to look then at Shannon.'

'We quickly copped on in the *Star* that Shannon was the Manchester United of Irish sport. They were getting 8,000 people to games and winning the AIL, and Garryowen jealousy would come across the next time the sides met.

'I remember being at one packed out match where Paul McMahon had scored the winning try, and he had just transferred over from Young Munster to Shannon. That whole breeding ground and sense of passion and belief is what is inherited by Munster fans from the AIL. They might not go to the AIL as much as they used to but the passion is still there, supporting the province. That said, I don't know how much the success of the province has impacted on the club teams.'

There is a current view amongst rugby pundits that the introduction of professionalism had a detrimental effect on the club scene. At first the AIL teams began funnelling money into the top players, and the Chelsea mentality took over—the more you spent, the better you were.

However, the knock-on effect was that the provinces were then taking the better players off the clubs and despite having the elite of Irish rugby on the books, they rarely played for their home clubs. As a result, many clubs quickly ran out of money with the top players signing for the provinces instead of the Shannons and Galwegians.

However, not all journalists buy into this apocalyptic vision of the Irish club scene. According to Foley, club rugby in Munster is still as strong as ever, almost mirroring the successes of the provincial team.

'If you look at this season they have four teams in the top flight, eight teams in the second flight and four teams in the third flight. And you would bet your life that Youghal will come up this year, much like Nenagh Ormond last year or Bruff before them.

'I always say to people at Munster games—watch the Shannon banners and watch the peripheral banners of fans outside of the province. I mean whether you like it or not, main street Kilkenny people are Munster fans, as are Portlaoise.

'Look at the rise of a team like Athlone Buccaneers. They are a phenomenal case study in their own right. They have clearly benefited from their position in the pale of Munster, just coming outside of the boundaries. There is no other situation where a team outside of Munster could have done so well; Waterpark, Clonakilty and Bruff are all feeding out of that positive vibe that is alive in their province at the moment.'

Caught somewhere between Connaught, Leinster and Munster, the Buccs have managed to drum up incredible support and have developed an intense survival instinct that bears remarkable likeness to any of the traditional Munster teams in the AIL.

'I would think most Buccaneers supporters are Munster supporters. Munster's European Cup run used all of this passion and married it with the cream of the crop of players from the AIL to produce this rollercoaster ride that is their quest for glory. I don't know, maybe this longing for tickets and going to away matches, that a type of person from a soccer background wouldn't do, and not only that, but wanted to do it with his wife or girlfriend, only added to the mix. The profile of the Munster fan is simply something different and is just nothing like the Shamrock Rovers fan in Europe or the Irish fan at Italia '90.'

'Munster appears to have 14,000 home supporters for Thomond and 80,000 for when they are needed elsewhere; you tell me any other club in the world that has that sort of following. And when you look at the most important players for Munster over the Heineken Cup campaign, they all starred in the AIL and in reality that is where they were noticed.

'They haven't won it before now because Declan Kidney was taken away at the wrong time; the Christian Cullen saga is unbelievable—to pay top dollar for the best full back in the world at the right side of the age of 30, only for him to get injured and injured again. People have pin pointed the fact that they have no backs but they could have bought three good backs for the price of Cullen.

'Horgan and Kelly are superb wingers and do exactly what Munster want; they cut in and recycle and rarely turn over ball. These two guys, I can hardly express how useful and how much part of the team these two extremely underrated players have been for Munster. What they have done away from home is that they go into contact and don't lose the ball, which is Munster's game plan. Granted, they are not international class wingers but they are top flight European backs who never let their side down and often pull it out of the bag.

'It has been a centre problem, and just as they seem to have righted that problem with the exciting new prospect of Barry Murphy, he gets injured against Ulster and is ruled out for the season. I mean, at any time this year they have had 11 players either on the Irish first team or squad, so they are not short of class.

'But aside from that they always had that little bit extra, those certain key players who have lifted them above the rabble in games they should be winning, and carried them to heights above when they should undoubtedly be losing.'

One such man for Foley is Mick Galwey.

'Galwey's ability to speak to people is absolutely outstanding and at times underrated. So when they were winning their first match away from home in Italy, and when he describes the steps, as that was the first time we won away, and the first time we won in France, that was a quarter-final; he never looked at the whole of the journey but took each step as it came and convinced the players to do the same.

'He could communicate that to others and he and Anthony Foley, who has a great rugby brain, understood exactly where Galwey was at, and could then communicate that to John Hayes. 'Gallaimh' could make the right call in a pressure situation. That might have been to throw the ball to a particular person in a crucial lineout situation, and it may look like an easy and obvious thing to those sitting in the stand, but sometimes that can be the hardest call of all.

'But Galwey performed another crucial function for Munster Rugby; he was a people's captain. He would talk to the man on the ditch as quickly as the paddy in the press box and knew that respect went both ways.

'The fact of the matter was that Munster was nothing without their legions of fans and Galwey knew this, and like a politician on Election Day he was willing to share himself all around, all the time. Mick Galwey was the fulcrum of the Munster team, the liaison amongst fans, press, management and players.

'You see things and you go "Oh my God, that just sums the man up completely," explains Foley.

'I was on a charter plane going to a match in France and we were in with the team and the fans. We had no sooner taken off when Mick had opened up his seat belt and was wandering down to the fans for a chat. "How are you doing, I'm Mick Galwey, who are you?" you would here him say in his loud but soft voice.

'The fan would tell him who he was and maybe get an autograph or a picture, and you would hear Mick saying, "I'm really pleased you could come." I can still hear him chatting away, he was simply the best. And he would spend the whole flight making his way through all the fans on the plane making each one feel part of the Munster set up.

'And on the way home after the win he was at the same sort of thing, signing everything, thanking everybody, and he spent the whole flight back thanking the fans. I mean other people can sign autographs and not mean it. I saw a Leinster captain recently give a speech on a plane, thanking the fans on board through the intercom. It was a fairly average speech. A Galwey speech always involves the fans, and that was his gift and why he was so important in the generating of this phenomenon that is Munster rugby.'

Another of Munster's crucial players for Foley is the man who shares his surname, Anthony 'Axel' Foley. Foley has been a long serving member of Munster and like Galwey, has been there from the off of the journey. But for the *Star* journalist he is the vital cog in the Munster forward machine.

'Anthony Foley is Ireland's top scorer in Heineken Cup rugby. Obviously the higher the standard of rugby you go to, the higher scorers tend to be backs, and it is a great testament to Foley that he is out-scoring top class international backlines. I take for my example the Six Nations. The top scorer of the six nations is invariably a back, except for last year when Wales' Martin Williams snuck it.

'But when you look at a team on paper, you are not looking for your Number 8 to be a prolific, consistent try scorer, yet that's what Foley is. I mean, in the Heineken Cup he has scored more tries than Dennis Hickey, a top class international winger and one of Ireland's top try scorers. More tries than Brian O' Driscoll, Ireland's top try scorer, in this competition.'

Foley may not have had the oratory skills that 'Gallaimh' had, but he knows how to put the standard down and the others know that when you have the ball you run towards him and near him and he will look after things.

But when thinking of the future and of this year's incredible and historic campaign one man stands out like a jolly ginger giant; the brilliant, the incredible, the amazing Paul O'Connell.

He quite simply has taken Munster, Ireland and Europe by storm. A shy, retiring man he may be off the pitch, but he is without doubt a leader and giant on it. In fact his reputation has at times gotten the better of him, never more than when he played for the Lions last year in their ill-fated tour of New Zealand.

The man-giant O'Connell was being touted as the next Martin Johnson, a man who could inspire miracles and take the mighty All Blacks to school.

However O'Connell did not enjoy the wealth of talent that surrounded Johnson during his World Cup win, or Lions victory in South Africa. For this reason, the second row would come under some fierce media scrutiny from the British press, and return home as a national hero but with a damaged reputation internationally. Something he would soon rectify.

During the 2006 Six Nations campaign, O'Connell would personally attempt to destroy all opposition in both the tight and the loose, demolishing the much touted English, Welsh and French lineouts. This was done with a consistency that translated to his provincial form that led Munster through the group stages and onto the knockout competition of the Heineken Cup.

According to Foley, O'Connell is the best thing to happen to Munster and Ireland since Keith Wood.

'Paul O'Connell is Alexander the Great, in one way the complete opposite of Galwey as a player, but so similar as a person. O'Connell's ability to have a Master's degree in winning always comes through in his rugby. Don't forget, this is a very bright man who has played sport at the top level in many different disciplines, particularly in golf and swimming.

'I met his father, who was also a very bright man, and he led me to believe that Paul could probably do a PHD on winning and still get all the spelling right, the tenses and grammar correct, and maybe in French for good measure. His interviews are worth watching for their lack of clichés, as he attempts to articulate to mere journalists what is actually going on both on and off the pitch. He has this incredible standard of perfection and calmness for a man who wouldn't think twice about ripping your head off on a pitch.

'Yet this is a man you would quite happily leave minding your five year old child, and on your return find out she had become a three handicap golfer. He simply has standards that nobody in international soccer or in any other discipline has, and that transcends to his play.

'The other players respond to this in a way that they did to 'Gallaimh' before him, continuing the trend of self belief and pride that keeps them winning miracle matches. And while the points kicker and the scrum-half are all important components to this team, throughout the Cup for me these players epitomise Munster and their journey in Europe. They are one of the main elements of this Munster phenomenon.'

MUNSTER RUGBY FACT:

The Munster Crest

The 'three crowns' emblem used by Munster was a common symbol throughout medieval Europe. It is connected with the story of the three wise men of the New Testament Gospel of St Matthew. It was a symbol of the English lordship of Ireland until replaced during the reign of Henry VIII.

In 2003 the Munster crest was revamped to include a stag's head (an animal associated with Munster folklore as far back as the 11th century). Said to be an aggressive and competitive animal, the stag represents very well the spirit of Munster rugby.

Photo © Press 22

The day a legend was born; 31 October 1978. Up to 100,000 jubilant fans claim to have turned up to watch the men of Munster take on the mighty All Blacks and win with a tremendous display of courage, skill and desire, paving the way for future generations to play with a self-belief that has become a trademark of Munster Rugby. The achievement has been immortalised in books, songs, and plays, and has taken on a mythical status.

Photo © Sportsfile

Following the lines of Dion O'Cuinneagain, honorary Irishman Trevor Halstead makes another telling break.

Mick Galwey makes one of his trademark inspirational charges against Bourgoin while a fresh faced Anthony Foley looks on.

Dennis Leamy storms past Craig Quinnell for Munster against the Cardiff Blues.

Mick O'Driscoll soars high into the night sky to claim a lineout ball against the Gwent Dragons, as Peter Stringer waits to receive.

Photo © Press 22

Peter Stringer uses his low centre of gravity to good effect against the Newport Gwent Dragons after Leamy destroys another Welsh ruck.

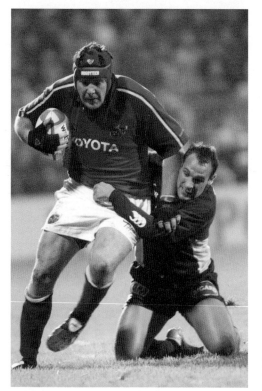

Munster Captain Anthony Foley makes the hard yards against Castres.

Photo © Press 22

A Newport Gwent Dragon runs into a red
brick wall consisting of Denis Leamy and
Mick O'Driscoll.

Anthony Horgan takes a thumping tackle from Cardiff flanker Martin Williams.

Anthony Foley brushes off wee
Shane Williams bursting for the
white wash against the Neath
Swansea Ospreys.

The red army of Munster fans at Bourgoin start the journey that will eventually
herald the Heineken Cup.

The Young Munster forward line preparing for a scrum. The Munster squad comprises of players from all over the province and from teams that recognise no class system; Clonakilty, Cork Constitution, Dolphin, Garryowen, Highfield, Midleton, Old Crescent, Shannon, Sundays Well, Thomond, UL Bohemians, Waterpark and Young Munster.

Photo © Press 22

Photo © Press 22

Ex-Munster coach Alan Gaffney managed to bring Munster their first piece of European silverware in years.

Peter Clohessy and the Munster scrum take the
strain against the might of London Wasps and
England captain Lawrence Dallaglio.

The opposition need four arms each to fend off the
Munster challenge of seasoned wing John Kelly.

'It is not the brilliance of their back play but the primal ferocity of the Galwey gang up front that drives Munster rugby to the hearts and minds of all.'
– Stuart Barnes on the Munster Machine

Chapter 5: Mick Galwey

People always say that you should never meet your heroes because you will always be disappointed that they are not what you made them out to be in your mind. But when it comes to rugby, what makes you a hero is your performance on the pitch, which is in full view of the world. When it comes to heroes of the Munster rugby variety, they don't come much bigger than Kerry man Mick Galwey.

The first time I saw 'Gallaimh' in the flesh was in Kitty O'Shea's in Paris in 2002 after Ireland had received a proper throttling. In person he is a giant, but a gentle one, with a kind word for every fan and a willingness to please.

Whilst standing at the thronged bar waiting almost ten minutes to order a pair of €10 pints, the sea of punters suddenly began to part and Mick arrived to put in his drink order. Straight away the bar staff rushed to his side and took the order. Just as he was about to finish he turned his granite-like gaze over to me and asked, 'What are you waiting for lad?'

I told him my order, which he called, and refused to accept payment. Next thing, his round of drinks came, which must have totalled €100, and with a wicked grin he quipped, 'Your shout next,' and then disappeared into the crowd again. Thankfully he never came to collect, but certainly put paid to the idiom on meeting your heroes. For me there was only one dead cert for this book when it came to players and their views on Munster's extraordinary relationship with the Heineken Cup. First on the list, Galwey is now synonymous with Munster's never-ending search for European glory. He has fronted countless programmes and his love for both the competition and the fans that follow the team is the stuff of many Limerick bar yarns.

His heroics for Ireland and Munster have made him a household name in every county in the country and his ferocity and never-say-die spirit made him a formidable opponent abroad.

Meeting in the Quality Inn by the new Docklands development, Mick Galwey had rerouted some of his precious time away from coaching the national club team in order to talk to me. Apart from that time in Paris, I had met Galwey on one other occasion, but I decided against bringing up the clobbering I received from him in Kilkenny two years prior to that. But you could tell he remembered.

Despite his new career in coaching both Shannon and the amateur national team, it is obvious where Mick's heart will always lie. Even when he first moved from Kerry to Limerick, his sights were entirely focused on the red jersey of Munster.

'I would have played under age rugby for Munster back in 1985, for the U18s in a game against Ulster played in the Railway Union Grounds in Sandymount in Dublin. I suppose back then I didn't realise the total importance of playing for my province.

Not that I didn't think it was great, and the one thing that hooked me was of the course the fact that they beat the All Blacks, and that I was now part of that history and that pride. 1987 was the first time that I played with the senior side and got my first cap.'

But the step up from club rugby was bigger back in the amateur day than it is now. There were no academies or development programmes designed to ease players into the provincial level. Instead, Galwey relied on a couple of old hands to help him adjust.

'Well I suppose back then it was huge and once you found yourself playing for Munster you felt like you were in the shop window as regards international success and club status. Once I started playing rugby and joined Shannon from Castle Island, the next step was obviously to try and make that interprovincial team.

'At Shannon I was lucky enough to be playing with Colm Tucker and Ginger McLaughlin who had both played against New Zealand. They were internationals, they were Lions. So playing with players like that, who were involved with those great teams and had such experience helped me grow as a player, and I suppose in a way pushed me towards the Munster jersey.

'That meant an awful lot to me. The one great thing about Munster, and especially back then, was not the three interprovincials but the games against the touring sides, and my first big game for Munster was against the All Blacks in 1989. It was seen as like the return fixture because the last time we had played them they had lost.

'We played in Cork but they beat us well on the day, 31-19 I think, but to have played against the All Blacks, who were world champions at the time, was just fantastic. Having come through that game with only minor injuries I simply said to myself, the sky is the limit, and went for everything.

'Mind you, I think now that if one of the big three teams in the Southern Hemisphere—New Zealand, Australia or South Africa—decided to come to Ireland in the morning and play the four provinces and then play Ireland it would be great for Irish rugby.

'I mean, to see the current team of Munster players play Graham Henry's First 15 in Thomond would be special. Like, you can talk about New Zealand playing any team and playing in an any venue, but a rematch of that infamous match in '78 would just be fantastic; and let them bring all their big boys, I wouldn't back against Munster. I guess that sums up what I believe about Munster. I believe that they could beat the current All Blacks in Thomond Park.'

This wasn't the first time I had heard such confidence in Munster, and it wouldn't be the last; that desire and belief has always been a vital part of the team and has brought them to where they are now, at the summit of European rugby. It has always been there, Galwey argues, and the sky really was the limit for the talented second row. Not long after his Munster caps came Irish caps and with that his arrival onto the world stage of rugby. But by 1995 something was stirring in the think-tanks of the ERC that would change Galwey's life forever—the Heineken Cup.

'The Heineken Cup was and is huge, and when it first started it was incredible. I remember the first year, the first European game we played was against Swansea in Thomond Park, and we should have been beaten that day. They were a good side, a professional Welsh outfit in the amateur days, and they should have whipped us off the park. But in fairness, a last minute try and we sneaked the game, but they out-scrummaged us, out-tackled us, and actually beat us in every aspect but the scoreboard.

'Then we played Castres away, and I think we had to play them three times before we got an away win, and we struggled again in our next match. But the following season, Wasps came to Thomond Park and they had Dallaglio and Tuigamala, Damien Cronin, Andy Reid, a star studded international team, and we put 50 points on them.

'That game proved to me that there was something special about that competition and planted the seed that said, "Wait a minute here, if we can beat these guys we can go on and win the whole thing."

'When you think about the great players that have come to Thomond Park it's amazing. Like the Saracens side whom we beat 31-13, and they had World Cup winning Captain Francois Pienar on their team. With him came Richard Hill, Tony Diprose, Scott Murray and Danny Grewcock, who are still going well, and in the front row you had Paul Wallace and Daniel Schutte, who is now the Leicester hooker, and Julien White. That was a class pack and they had the backs to match. They were the best side to come to Thomond Park, and we beat them.

'Games like that and star-studded sides like Gloucester in the miracle match, or whatever you want to call it, don't happen by fluke. There is something special and completely out of the ordinary when a team like Munster can make these great sides look very, very average, while the Munster boys play above themselves.

'That is one of the great things about this competition; that it has kept the professional game at this level of intense passion and spirit, and I don't think that will ever go. Take Thomond Park, and look at it when there is nobody in it, and it looks very ordinary, a big elephant of a concrete jungle. But you put a home crowd there on the night of a must-win game and there is no better place to play rugby in the world.'

But while Mick is quick to list Thomond Park and the fans as part of Munster, he is leaving out one of the most obvious factors that makes the Munster phenomenon—Mick Galwey.

With the departure of the mercurial Keith Wood after the 2000 campaign, the players and fans desperately sought a new talismanic leader. They found one in 'Gallaimh'.

His charismatic manner allowed for a healthy relationship with referees, his aggressive and inspiring play on the pitch led others, and his rapport with the Thomond faithful guaranteed a packed house whatever the game. But playing down his pivotal role, Galwey is quick to point out that it is more a pride issue than a leadership factor that helps Munster win. Oh, and also that Munster don't exactly win every match—even when they are the better team.

'The will to win was huge, and now, thankfully, I have moved on and other great heroes have retired and passed on that jersey to new players, and nobody wants to be the team that loses in Thomond. Some people might say that is a lot of pressure but I don't. I think it brings out the best in people, and if you aren't scared of losing then you will never play above yourself.

'Having that feeling is a great motivator and it's not some great weight on your back. It's what Munster have at the moment and I believe is why they are doing so well.'

But that fear did not help them win their first Heineken Cup final. Worse still that nearly every pundit and player, including Galwey, has since admitted Northampton were there for the taking. If you look at the seven years of the Heineken Cup, it is rare that a team will be beaten when they score the only try of the game. And it was a great try, but still at the end of the game the scoreboard read 9-8 in favour of the Saints.

'I know looking back at that match that it was a game we should have won. That was a game we were good enough to win but didn't. We will never go out in a game again and not score like that. Ronan O'Gara was averaging 17-18 points a match and didn't score in the final, through no fault of his own, because we didn't produce those chances. I mean, we scored the only try of the match and on any other day we would have put them away.'

And it was a textbook, blackboard try. Kidney had noticed that their right winger would always stay about five metres out of position, as if he was worried about a blind side break. This left Dom Malone, the scrum half, with a lot of ground to cover and he often found himself on the wrong side of the scrum;. The team had been waiting for that to happen all day and sure enough it happened.

When they scored it, they were one try to nil up and beginning to take control of the game, but then Mick Galwey was put in the sin bin. They lost their key man at a crucial time and were forced to go into defensive mode. By the time they had braved the storm and Galwey returned, they were forced to go into panic mode as time was running out and they had only ten minutes to score.

'It just didn't work for us that day and Lady Luck deserted us because Northampton were a good side, but they weren't as good as the Leicester side that beat us in the Millennium Stadium, yet that was a game that we could have won also. It was heartbreaking for us, especially when we looked around the stadium and saw the fans still singing and chanting. They are a very special part of this team.'

However, sometimes factors other than luck conspired to wrench the silver cup away from Galwey's grasp. That one incident that all Munster fans kept looking back at, against Leicester at the

Millennium Stadium in 2001, was to mar the whole match and the whole occasion.

In the final moments of the game, with Munster trailing but still in with a great chance, they had the Leicester Tigers pinned to their line. Dangerously close to a penalty try, and with a scrum in front of the post, it looked like Munster were finally going to win the championship. Then, in a moment of either madness or brilliance, opposition flanker and seasoned English international Neil Back slapped the ball out of Peter Stringer's hands into the Leicester side of the scrum.

Munster lost another final thanks to the hand of Back. While Galwey prefers not to dwell too long on the incident, he still has issues with the canny wing forward.

'I certainly look back on it and say to myself, well it certainly was an important incident and if it hadn't happened that way well you never know. Because we had a planned move from that scrum; Anthony Foley breaks and passes to Peter Stringer and he puts it back into David Wallace and you know I had visions of us scoring under the posts with Ronan O'Gara kicking the conversion. Match over. But it didn't happen that way.

'I was disappointed at the time because the touch judge didn't do anything and Neil Back straight away afterward said he would have done anything to win the match, which I suppose you could live with. But then two months later he apologised about it, which to me was a bit of a kick in the teeth. To me he should either never have apologised or apologised straight away, but don't rub salt in the wound, you know.

'He made a statement at the time, which was a fairly harsh one, that he did what he had to do for Leicester, and that was fair enough, but to turn around months later and say what he did—that was horrible.

'I mean, it was a funny thing with that incident, and I have letters at home sent from Leicester supporters saying that they wanted to give back their jerseys, that this wasn't Leicester's final because they didn't win it. Okay, they won it because they were leading at the time, but they denied us from scoring.

'In the end though, they were a good side, and I couldn't stand here and tell you that we were a better team than Leicester, but the one thing I can say is that on our day we could beat anybody. Now our day didn't always come but honestly, and I don't say this lightly, we could beat anybody and you can throw the All Blacks into that.'

Again there is the mention of the top team in the world, such is the confidence and belief within Munster, and this has only multiplied since the ghosts of that fateful day have finally been laid to rest.

Mick Galwey is no longer the inspirational leader of the Munster pack. He has passed on that mantle to the worthy figure of Paul O'Connell and he has always been confident that this crop of players have had what it takes to complete the journey he started out on ten years ago. Even though I spoke to him before the knockout games, he spoke almost as if Munster were destined to win.

'For the last eight years we have qualified for the quarter-finals and that in itself is phenomenal. To come out of your group every year is a tough task, and then to get to the semi-finals and twice to the final is fantastic. And when you think about it, once you are out of your group you need to win only three games to win the Heineken Cup. Okay, it's against good opposition and you could be away from home, but once you lay well and you have that bit of luck you always have a shot.

'Now, I think they are very close, and even this time around a lot has to do with injuries, and if Munster have their full squad to the very end then you'd have to back them. But we'll say, what if John Hayes got injured, or Paul O'Connell, then it gets harder.

'Mind you Paul O'Connell is replaceable in Munster, we have back up there. I mean, probably the best second row in the world is replaceable in Munster, but John Hayes isn't. He isn't replaceable for Ireland or Munster, and that is the harsh fact because there is a shortage of good props. But saying that, I think they are close and I certainly wouldn't be writing them off this year.

They were 40-1 before the Castres away game and that was a great bet and I had a bit of a flutter myself. Nothing serious, but it was good odds.' So what did playing for Munster mean for Galwey, who has starred for his country and the Lions? Surely the Six Nations tries and the victories in Lansdowne are the shining lights in his glittering career? Of course not. 'It means everything to play for Munster, and when I say that I actually mean everything. Like, people ask me what is my proudest moment in sport and mine is captaining Munster, leading them onto the pitch. Ok, you can talk about your Heineken Cup finals and you can talk about the great matches away, but running onto the pitch at Thomond Park, leading your team out, well there is simply nothing better than that. And I did it as a captain and as a player, and the lift you get is unbelievable. It just brings you up.

'What I would say to anybody who is interested in playing for the province, is that their goal should be to play a Heineken Cup game in Thomond Park. Of course everyone wants to play for their country, and that is a great honour, but playing Heineken Cup for

Munster in Thomond Park is certainly up there with the best of them. There is nothing up there to touch it.

'I've been lucky enough when it comes to sport. I've played with Kerry in All Ireland finals in Croke Park, and I am a great sports fan in general and follow all sports, but playing for Munster is simply something special.'

And with that Mick sat back, sipped the end of his coffee, and the interview was finished. 'If you need anything else give me a shout,' he added before heading off to meet his international charges. And like that, he was gone, to mastermind another victory at Lansdowne Road. This time, however he would have to play his part from the unfamiliar confines of the West Stand.

And what are the chances of him doing the same for a Munster team in a Heineken Cup final? Even at odds of 40-1, he told me, I shouldn't bet against it.

MUNSTER RUGBY FACT:

Record attendances

Munster have played in all games holding attendance records in the knock-out stages of the Heineken Cup. These are:

■ The final, 2002, v Leicester, at the Millennium Stadium, Cardiff – 74,600

■ The semi-final, 2004, v London Wasps, Lansdowne Road, Dublin – 49,500

■ The quarter-final, 2006, v Perpignan, Lansdowne Road, Dublin – 49,500

■ The 2005 quarter-final against Biarritz in Estadio Anoeta, across the border in San Sebastian, with an attendance of 32,000 also set the record for the biggest rugby match ever played in Spain.

**'They may well be the greatest team never to win the European cup and I think that is a real possibility.'
– George Hook**

Chapter 6: Munster Rugby; the tradition and history

One of the cruellest factors that I believe has affected the men from Munster lies in the appointing of national, regional and quasi-national radio licences by the Broadcasting Commission of Ireland. Essentially what the BCI has done is deprive fans and fanatics of 'The Right Hook' and its controversial presenter, the larger than life George Hook.

For now, only available in Dublin and over Chorus Digital in some remote areas of the country, Hook daily extols his virtues on the population of our nation's capital with vim and vigour. Newstalk is set to spread over the airwaves of the nation as a whole by late autumn, but Dubliners have a head start in getting to know this colourful man and his opinions.

Without doubt his keenest insights are evident when he casts his cold eye on the game of rugby, and he has on many an occasion ruffled the feathers of the province's plumage.

A regular pundit with RTÉ and the *Sunday Independent*, Hook has made a name for himself with his unwavering dedication to the cold hard truth. His willingness to put the boot in when necessary has managed to generate an incredible love-hate relationship with the Munster fans.

Yet beneath this hardened exterior lies a loyal and unwavering love for a game that he has devoted most of his life to, through playing and coaching.

Of course, meeting a man like that can be an intimidating process and sitting in the busy restaurant of the Lansdowne Hotel on Baggot Street I mulled over my questions carefully. Nothing would appear worse than coming across as a sycophantic die-hard searching for a cheap line for this book.

And as Hook strolled in the door, followed straight away by a presence that almost made him seem double his size, I realised that I was not going to get an interview but an education.

The first thing that struck me about him was his size: he is an incredibly tall man. The second was his openness. He met me on the afternoon of his wedding anniversary, and after a conference in the Regency Airport Hotel.

I couldn't begrudge him the plate of chicken curry and the pint of Heineken he devoured during the discussion. He got right into the subject at hand.

'There is a belief that Munster rugby is about the Heineken Cup and it's not,' he told me, when I presented him with my thesis on the phenomenon theory.

'Munster rugby has had this extraordinary tradition since World War II. If you look at the history of touring sides coming to this country since that time, these touring sides would have always beaten Ireland but the match in Munster was always an astonishing game. And the records show that the All Blacks in the 1970s and the South Africans in the 1960s and even the Aussies in the 1970s all lost in some amazing matches.

'At that point Munster only played three matches a year, which was the old interprovincial championship against the other three provinces, so once every three or four years a touring side would come, play the match in Thomond park and people would be hanging out of the rafters.

'I was there in the mid-1950s when Munster played the All Blacks in Cork and I have pictures of the crowd that day, and you just wouldn't see that sort of thing again; probably for health and safety reasons. But they were hanging out of the stands, up on the roof, anything you could do to see the game.

'So Munster always had the special underdog tradition of playing against the foreign teams and winning and in many ways this has been replaced now by the Heineken Cup.'

Not to be discouraged and fairly sure that there is in fact a substantial X-factor attached to the mighty Munster men, I pressed him again. This time Hook was more receptive to both the theory and the competition.

'It's quite difficult to quantify and I'm pretty certain there is no one specific reason behind this phenomenon, but you put this huge tradition together and mix it with Munster as underdogs and maybe that is it.

'There has always been the culture of the underdog in Munster Rugby so in the old amateur days when they picked the Irish team there were five selectors: two from Ulster, two from Leinster, and one from Munster. So, Munster always felt like they had gotten a raw deal.

'And as a result, every time the Irish team was announced the Cork Examiner went bananas about whoever didn't get a cap and I'm sure the same happened with the *Limerick Leader*. The people of Cork and Limerick would have developed this underdog culture of "everybody is against us" and we simply can't get a fair deal down here. I think that is a very important thing to understand—this underlying, brooding culture of the underdog. I think that is still the case today.

'The game against the All Blacks in 1978 is now immortalised in song and story and play and all that sort of thing but the reality of it is that they could have beaten a touring side almost every time since World War II. So 1978 was always going to happen, it was just a case of when, and those 15 guys are heroes. But again those players are part of a tradition who laid down the law and played for their lives.

'I remember a game against South Africa and the players just wouldn't leave the field injured, and they were bloodied, battered and beaten, wrapped in bandages but still kicking the living shit out of the Springboks, who were one of the best touring sides at the time.

'So then along comes the Heineken Cup and suddenly Munster start playing other teams in Europe, and at the start they didn't do very well. I mean, if you study the early years before 1999/2000, they rarely won away and their home form at times left a lot to be desired—getting continually hockeyed by French teams. And then what really happened was Declan Kidney arrived and brought an organisation and discipline to the Munster outfit.'

Hook has always been respectful of Declan Kidney through his punditry, and while not always complimentary of his strategy on the day, it is obvious there is a level of appreciation garnered from Hook's own coaching days, be it from the time he coached Queens University's under 20 side to victory or when he coached Connaught, but definitely Hook knows his stuff.

'I'm not saying that Kidney was necessarily a great coach but that he created this level of discipline that Munster has craved. They always had the fire in the belly but needed the organisation.

'The other thing was that more and more of the games began to be played in Thomond Park. Thomond Park is a unique place in world rugby, like, the crowd staying silent for every kick, irrespective of who is kicking. I can remember Stade Français playing in Thomond Park and Dominguez having a kick to effectively win the match, and the crowd were still silent—that is simply extraordinary.'

Of course, George Hook is a Cork man, and as much a fan of tripe and drisheen as of rugby as a whole. So what of Thomond's poorer cousin that lies within the constituency of 'De Banks' of the Lee: Musgrave Park? Time and time again fans will wag their heads ominously if a game is moved south, citing all kinds of figures and facts. Of course, for a pragmatist like Hook, this is more a case of fishwives' tales and a pinch of Limerick's ascendancy over Cork.

'All of this is about tradition; rugby in Munster has always been different. Rugby in Ulster, Leinster and Connaught is about rugby in the province but rugby in Munster is about two competing cities: Limerick and Cork. Munster rugby is divided into the North Munster branch and the South Munster branch, and no other branch in Ireland has that situation.'

'Cork and Limerick have always been competing, always, and Munster teams would have to travel to Mallow or far flung places in order to find a neutral ground to train. So there was always that kind of internal warfare but Limerick in fact was the perfect place to play rugby.

'If someone had ever sat down and employed sociologists, architects and anthropologists and said, "Now, out you go and find the perfect place in the world to build a rugby stadium that identifies with the population", then they would have come back with Limerick. The reason for this is that it is one of the few and maybe the only city in the world where the game crosses all divides.

'Rugby has always been a middle class game. Even in Wales where they would talk about miners and steelworkers in villages turning out for the local sides, it was still played in the grammar schools. Munster was different and you also had the rich tapestry of the clubs, and each one represented something different.'

Even today when you play rugby down in Limerick, the kind of people who played for Garryowen were quite different from the people who played for Young Munster or Shannon. Personally, I can remember not getting a kicking, punching or gouging when I lined out against Garryowen, as opposed to Shannon or Munster, but maybe that was because I was playing for a Dublin 4 club. There was no rivalry.

Still, Hook is adamant that the Munster team managed something that neither the Good Friday Agreement nor Bill Clinton could manage—to unite two warring factions.

'You had a team that crossed all boundaries, you had a ground with an extraordinary tradition, and you had a city that was going to identify with rugby. And remember, no other city in the country identifies with rugby as much, not even Belfast. There are as many people who go to Windsor Park to watch soccer teams as go to Ravenhill—there is nowhere else where the entire city is part of the one team only.

'Now there is another thing that happens in sport. If you were to ask somebody why the Ryder Cup suddenly became the biggest sporting event in the world when just a couple of decades ago

Europe were constantly getting hammered by the US; what would the answer be? How did that happen?'

'Accident!' I guessed.

'Faldo, Woosnam, Ballesteros and Langer were all born within 12 months of each other, so there was essentially the conjoining of the stars to produce these four guys who would become the spine of the European team that was to beat America. Now, exactly the same thing happened in Munster rugby. For example, Munster has always been able to produce forwards but what it needed was a fly half, and then O'Gara arrived.'

And of course along with him came the new great white and ginger hope of Irish rugby, Paul O'Connell. Also worth more than a mention are Donnacha O'Callaghan, Peter Stringer and Marcus Horan. This quintet of key players is as much a part of Munster's success as the grounds or the history or tradition. But as anybody who reads his column, listens to his radio show, or watches him on TV knows, Hook rates 'ROG', or Ronan O'Gara to the rest of us.

'The game of rugby, despite everything that is written about it, is a game about kicking points, and he kicks points. Again, in history, when you go back, Munster had Nick English or Dan Daly, so through all the good periods they have had a good out half. Then the whole charismatic element just arrived into the team with players like Galwey.'

'He was a clever man and he unashamedly used his relationship with the crowd to great effect. I really think that Galwey's part in it has been completely undersold in that he had the ability to connect with the people as the spiritual leader of the team.'

Mick Galwey simply had an inspiring presence. When I talked to him about this book, I could see that he remembered me from somewhere. I certainly remembered him. It was two years ago, and

I was lining out for Monkstown to play a struggling Kilkenny Junior side.

The Cats hadn't won any of their previous four games and we were a bit cocky about doling out a hiding, so much so that one or two players may have indulged in a beverage or two the night before. Imagine my surprise and horror when our opponents were led out by none other than Mick Galwey.

To nobody's surprise he single-handedly beat us about the park and even managed to give me a personal welcome with a life-changing tackle. Yet after the game a pint was bought and delivered by the now docile and gentle giant. It wasn't hard to see why he was so admired. My trip down memory lane was interrupted by Hook.

'Now suddenly you had a team with a spiritual leader, your typical hard Munster pack, a fly half who could kick goals, and all the ingredients were there for success in the Heineken Cup. The city was ready and the tradition was already laid down before them and it was now all about timing, and that's why they were successful.'

And here lies the nub, so to speak. If they had all these ingredients and great players, why did they have to wait so long to win?

As ever, Hook had the answers.

'Despite all the changes in coaching and rules and everything else, the scrum remains the fulcrum in rugby, and Munster has never had a scrum to match the rest of their parts. They lost to Northampton because Northampton bullied them up front; they lost to Leicester because they bullied them up front. So ultimately teams began to learn through the Heineken Cup campaign that if you want to beat Munster, you must bully them. Teams that could do this won, and those that couldn't, lost.

'Munster were always perfect for the European competition because French teams would always have a soft mental underbelly, by and large. Therefore, the strongest team mentally was always beating teams who were flawed mentally, even though on paper they should be losing. That is why Munster did so well against French teams and at home in Thomond Park.

'The reason they lost was because they never had a backline to match the pack. They were always short of pace in the middle of the field; always, always short of a real world class strike runner at full back. That's why they signed Christian Cullen, but he never played.

'Munster were always nearly there, but like any team which lacks a few vital components, they kept falling at the final fence and in fact never rectified their situation, and that may in fact prevent them from ever winning the competition. They may well be the greatest team never to win the European Cup, and I think that is a real possibility.'

We all know now that this, thankfully, has not turned out to be the case, but hindsight is a fine thing and at the time Hook's words had an ominous ring to them.

Before the final in Cardiff this year, if you were to go over the history of the Heineken Cup and went through the top six games, Munster have played and won in at least four of them. And as long as they keep plugging away and producing these thrilling games Munster rugby will continue to be a cash cow for the industry, win or lose. And surely with this constant revenue pouring in they will be able to 'do a Chelsea' and buy success.

'This is not rocket science,' says Hook. 'This is about people associating with an ideal, and Munster is that romantic ideal,' he reveals after pondering over a black coffee.

'They have to get the back line moving and you saw that in the Sale match when Kidney brought Murphy in and suddenly there was verve in the team; pace and innovation there. He still didn't have enough pace out wide so he brought Dowling in, and he still struggles in the scrum. Ultimately, to be champions of Europe you have to be near perfect and the one thing about this competition that makes it a great sports competition is the list of winners.

'You look at the list of winners and you are by and large looking at the aristocrats of European rugby. You can't dismiss Northampton because they are at the bottom of the Premiership today. Anybody with any knowledge of English rugby will know that they are one of the great hearts of the game. Nearby Leicester are also there, and of course the French giants of Toulouse and Brive.

'For Munster to win this competition they have to be a great side and the Heineken Cup finds out every weakness eventually, be it by the quarter-finals, semis or final, and no amount of money will change that. Munster's weaknesses have been exposed, and yes of course it is cruel, but that is what becoming the champions of Europe is about. If it was easy then nobody would care.'

Still being a 'glass is half full' kind of guy, and with an opportunity to interview the big guy himself, I had to ask the next big question, which at the time was still in the forefront of every Irish rugby fan's mind: What then will it take to win this? They have the history, the grounds, the underdog mentality, the kicker, the leadership: so what is missing?

As ever, George Hook pulled no punches. 'I think if Munster win the European Cup it will be with a different team. And the reason I think this is because only once in my entire career as a television pundit have I lost my perspective, my neutrality. I watch rugby matches for RTE and I am unbelievably cold in my analysis. When Tom McGuirk gets excited when Munster score, and is punching his hand in the air, I am not. I am incredibly dispassionate because I think, I have to do this. I can't be a supporter. I am not a fan, I am an analyst.

'Only once did I lose that perspective, and that was when Munster played Wasps in the Cup semi-final at Lansdowne Road in 2004. It was an extraordinary situation and they had lost O'Gara so early on, and Holland had come in and kicked all the goals and they had scored the tries. There they were in an unlosable position, and they lost.

'And I don't think they lost because Wasps were better. I believe they lost because each and every Munster player was saying deep down, "Don't fucking tell me it's going to happen again, don't tell me the cup is going to be dashed from our lips."

'I think that these Munster men, despite all their heroics, are damaged. When they play at home they go on the pitch in front of their home supporters full of positive thoughts having done the impossible before and knowing they can do it again.

'I believe they went into the Wasps match at a point in the competition where they had previously lost, so there was a negative in their heads, and at that point they said, "Not fucking again," and sure enough they lost. At that point I just couldn't watch the match, and I was paid to watch the match and to write about it and talk about it on television, but I just couldn't do it.

'So I went out of the studio and I started looking out the window that overlooks the level crossing at Lansdowne Road for about six or seven minutes. Sure enough, when I came back the tables had turned and they had conceded the crucial try.'

This revelation concluded the interview and the meal, as George was ready to head home to his lovely wife Ingrid to celebrate their anniversary, but it left me with a strange mix of hope and despair. Hook had outlined the greatness of Munster Rugby as he saw it, but he didn't think they could win the Cup yet. Not this year. Most people doubted they would at the time, with such an uphill battle ahead, but still, anything could happen if you put a fully fit squad of top players and the support of the fans who make every game a home game, and every stadium another Thomond Park.

MUNSTER RUGBY FACT:

Tony Ward

Tony Ward, Munster legend and Irish international, also played soccer in the UEFA Cup, for Limerick FC against Southampton in the 1980s.

'In truth everything that Munster is, Leinster is not.' – George Hook

Chapter 7: The Thomond factor

In many ways we have come to the crux of the Munster argument, the *raison d'etre*: What is the Thomond factor and can it be translated to another ground?

When you look at the stadium in Limerick during the day, a concrete mass, devoid of personality and completely empty, it appears to be a very ordinary place. In fact, when you see the row of houses wedged into one of the corners and the under developed surroundings, there is no possible way you could think that this is the most formidable place to play in Europe, and possibly the world.

Yet when that stadium is filled to the brim with screaming Munster fans, all with an agenda and an inbuilt belief that this is their home and they will not lose, it becomes a gladiator's arena where, more often than not, they win.

It is an incredible asset to any team, be it in rugby union, hurling or soccer, to think that you can host a home game and know that the other team is going to face not only 15 players hell bent on putting their heads right up their arses, but also the most hostile home crowd known to man.

I am not for one minute suggesting any hints of racism or abusiveness from the Thomond faithful. This is evident in the respect given when the opposition's kicker is about to take aim at the posts. It is simply a level of support that is not garnered by other teams.

Attending Thomond Park on any Munster night is special, but to be there during a Heineken Cup game is to die for. Under the lights in Limerick, rain pouring down from the open heavens and the red Munster men battling like gladiators in the local coliseum, devouring the countless Christian teams of Sale, Saracens or Gloucester—it is a sight to behold, and treasured, as the result is always the same; a home victory.

But of course many doubters who sit on stools in pubs in Dublin 4, sipping their 'Heino' do not understand this factor (even though they have had a brief taste of it in Lansdowne Road recently) and simply state that there is no wonderful reason for this phenomenon. And why would they?

No other team, especially not Leinster, has managed to re-create the remarkable success that now exists in the Limerick ground.

Friday night at Donnybrook boasts a similar sized crowd but fails to produce even a quarter of the zest and fervour of its sister ground. Because of this it is understandable to think that a form of envy has erupted between the provincial supporters when it comes to their home patches. Our support is bigger than yours, so to speak.

In many ways this feeling has spread to the teams and their coaching staffs.

Others prefer to dismiss it as simply a fleeting state of mind and that all grounds are equal in their support. But you ask any Munster player and they will impress on you what a big deal it is. It is a huge factor, but for practical reasons as well as any potentially mystical and superstitious ones.

One reason may be the unique design of the stadium, and while Cardiff it ain't, Donnybrook it never wants to be. Because of the design of the terraces, the crowds are right on top of the pitch and right down in the Ballynanty end it is always packed for big games. Playing there or supporting there, that atmosphere is completely unique as it almost feels like the crowd are down on top of you. It is as if the ground is the umbilical cord between the players and the crowd.

I was listening to the players talking after this year's remarkable Sale match, and both O'Connell and O'Callaghan were saying that before the match they experienced a noise level and a feeling that they had never felt before. It was because the crowd knew the importance of the Sale game, the decibel and noise level went up.

Thomond Park is the beating heart of Limerick and it was bursting the blood vessels, and hopes, of those Sale men as they stood in the Thomond arena waiting for the Lions. Sale had no chance that day and they were on a hiding to nothing.

Most people call it a turning point in the Sale game (but let's be fair—there was never a point to turn from as they were being beaten from the off) when there was a stoppage in play and the crowd simply turned on the Sale players. They sang and screamed and taunted them and the entire visiting team looked bewildered, staring around the place, wishing the ground would open up a nice big comfortable black hole that they could very quickly go and hide in.

The Munster team devoured the English giants that night, lifted continuously by the crowd, who were not just a 16th man, but a veritable potion of energy and emotion, a cocktail of which would drive any team to victory. And really until you experience it yourself you just cannot get your head around it—Thomond is not the place to play unless you are wearing red.

Of course, with such an exceptional weapon comes the secondary problem of reliance and the terrible problem of how to generate it at a different venue. As most people know, Munster also play at Musgrave Park in Cork, but the atmosphere is never the same there, nor are the games as electric.

Some people (those in charge of the coffers) ask the question: Is Thomond financially viable to sustain the money machine that is Munster Rugby Inc?

Well there is another ground in Limerick that could house twice as many fans, but it is the Gaelic grounds. In a different world, or even a different country, Munster would be playing in the GAA Park, as it has twice the capacity.

Would the tradition transfer along with the underdog history and the feeling of the crowd? Well, will we have a more sombre atmosphere when we rent out Croke Park for the Six Nations games? I don't believe so, and anybody who argues to the contrary has never been to Thomond or the Millennium Stadium when Munster are playing, and seen the spirit and will to win that has taken the boat, train or crop dusting plane over to support them.

Concrete and dirt don't have memories; what brings tradition alive is the people in the stadium and the band playing in the stands and the grass on the pitch. Thomond Park when it is empty isn't any different from any other ground in the world. What makes it special is that when it is full, it comes alive.

When you look at Thomond there really is something unbelievable going on.

There aren't too many grounds where you can be standing on the edge of a pitch and the crowd are only four feet away, roaring encouragement at you and good-natured abuse at the opposition. Or where the best team in the world could have a kick to win a game and they will get respectful silence. Somebody who boos in Thomond is out of place and the crowd will get on to them like they had just committed a crime, because it's just something special to be there.

As was proved in this year's final, you can translate that atmosphere anywhere, but the problem with Musgrave Park is simply that it is a smaller venue, and that is it. In reality, when Munster have played those games away from home and lost, it has little or nothing to do with the Thomond factor. The fans still travel. Sure, the home support is greater, but that only ignites the Munster passions and amplifies that 'cute-whorism'.

The lack of matches at Thomond Park was not the reason why Munster failed to win their first two finals or failed to qualify for countless others.

If you look at those games and the finals and semi-finals that they've lost, and look at the videos of the crowds, the grounds are packed, and with whom? Munster supporters.

They go to the UK and France bringing that same Thomond factor with them through storm and sunshine, and no matter how bad or disappointing the result, they are back queuing outside Thomond early the next season, booking tickets for the next match. There simply has never been a phenomenon like it in Irish sport and you can bet your last Euro that every morning, the directors of the European Rugby Cup Limited (ERC) thank their lucky stars that Munster exists, because they have made this tournament what it is. Even though Toulouse and Leicester are the Kingpins in terms of victories, Munster are what the ERC is all about.

It was a monkey that needed to be exorcised from their backs, but it was just reinforced in the Wasps semi-final and was only finally laid to rest this year when they buried a Leinster team that knocked out probably the best European rugby team on paper in Toulouse.

Granted, they just don't do things like that in Thomond Park and it is all well and good saying that the internationals are there and they should know better, but the team had perhaps too many painful memories.

Thomond Park offers a rare reality to any players, whether they love or hate it. The ground belongs to a working class community with history and pride attached. Lansdowne Road lies in the heart of Dublin 4 and is part-owned by a club that epitomises what Leinster Rugby used to be about. Theirs is an ethos which could never be adopted by the Munster faithful and is certainly in contrast with everything that the men in red stand for.

Which is why, during the semi-final this year, the Leinster men arrived to their home game to find that Thomond Park had in fact travelled up for the day. It was quite simply like a scene from a movie. Sure, if Mohamed won't come to the Mountain ... and the spirit of bricks, mortar, tradition and culture all managed to get tickets and redevelop Lansdowne Road for the afternoon.

The once cocky, quickly bewildered Leinster fans, were shepherded into the North Terrace, facing the South Terrace and surrounding stands with what was an ambush of red support. All Dublin 4 clubs had been infiltrated and plundered as half of the Leinster ticket allocation must have ended up in the hands of the Munster support who bellowed and bayed for their team.

Never had the Munster fans fought so hard to give their team the proper environment to beat the best backline in Irish rugby—with pure heart and brute force. Each time the play stopped, the Leinster players could be seen scanning the horizons, in desperate search for that one bit of blue in a sea of red that could inspire greatness. Sadly for them, they were engulfed in a wave of disappointment as their team was steamrolled by the Munster Machine that was fighting for survival in the knock-out stages of their favourite competition. They were hammered by a side who were responding to their fans who had managed to turn Lansdowne Road into a version of Thomond Park.

Both fans and players saw that spectre of past failures as it perched in the back of the North Terrace and proceeded, together, to put that ghost to bed.

It is unlikely after the job that was done there that day, that too many Leinster fans will take any joy in returning to Lansdowne for any home fixtures in next year's competition.

So this once again brings us back to the problem of discovering what the Thomond factor is. It is clear that it is an invaluable weapon for the Munster team and one they will not easily relinquish. And for a Munster team where the end result is much greater at times than the sum of its parts, it is fitting that this best explains the Thomond factor.

There are so many examples and anecdotes that can describe the atmosphere and cauldron-like adventure that is Thomond Park. Yet at the moment a battle for re-development is being waged in Limerick as the Branch aims to upgrade the home of Munster Inc to that of corporate status. And unashamedly they are willing to risk tearing down the holy shrine to the Munster tradition, all in the name of prosperity and maybe a hint of profit.

Why?

Because as we have seen on so many occasions Thomond is not just about the stadium or the people who once played there and the tradition they encompass. When they up the capacity, and quite possibly the seat prices, you will still get the same atmosphere and emotion pulsating from punter to players.

When the glass corporate boxes replace the rickety press box at the top of the stand, it will not diminish the wonderful desire and expectation of the old faithful bearing the wind and rain to will on their heroes.

And even when they turn the pitch so that the Ballynanty end is not where it once was, the team will keep on winning and more glory will surely be sought and demanded down in the south of Ireland.

Because in truth, Thomond is not bricks and mortar, it is an ideal, an example of the pure essence of sport that lives in this Munster franchise, through the devotion and love of the fans and their players.

And the reason why this didn't translate to other stadiums before this year is debatable. Maybe it was luck, divine inspiration, or maybe support is like a good team and the fans have in fact refined their craft and built and grown over that last few years before unleashing their best brand of chanting and singing, perfected over years of failures and almosts.

For let it be said once more, when Thomond Park is empty it is little more than a ramshackle stadium in the outskirts of a growing city. Even the great Millennium Stadium is simply a dome in the middle of Cardiff, a blip in the low skyline of the city. But when it is filled with the most unique crowd in the world, the devoted Munster fan, then it becomes something else completely.

It is the Thomond coliseum where dreams come true and Munster is not a belief but a birthright.

MUNSTER RUGBY FACT:

Ronan O'Gara

In the 05/06 season Ronan O'Gara scored a whopping 115 points making him the second highest points scorer in the competition. He scored one try, 22 conversions, only one drop goal but 21 penalties. The top scorer was Leinster's Felipe Contepomi who pipped the Munster man with 113 points.

Altogether since his debut in 1997/98, O'Gara has scored 764 points in the European competition.

'Munster seem to have 14,000 home supporters for Thomond and 80,000 for when they are needed elsewhere; you tell me any other club in the world that has that sort of following.'
– Derek Foley

Chapter 8: The Fans

For my mind there is no better supported rugby team in the world than Munster, a fact that has been demonstrated time and again since 1978. Anybody who still has the audacity or foolishness to doubt this devotion need only take a look at the 2006 Heineken Cup final. Despite the fact that they were always going to outnumber the opposition by at least six to one, some Munster fans took it upon themselves to be there by hook or by crook, just in case.

When the boats filled up, planes were chartered. When the planes were full they flew old crop dusting planes and one fan even travelled back from Brazil especially for the occasion. When Cardiff filled up, people stayed in Bristol and Cheltenham.

And what of those thousands of fans who couldn't get tickets or afford the spiralling air fares and accommodation? They took to the streets in the lashing rain to stand together and will their charges to victory. However, this part of the Munster phenomenon is not a new thing, it is simply one that has been refined over the years.

The love for the team originated in Limerick and gave birth to the red army. It is a different game in Limerick. When it comes to the fans there are simply no social barriers—it's docker or doctor. And according to former Munster star Tony Ward this is something he learned the first time he came to the town to play for Garryowen.

'It was after my second game in the Cup and I was thumping out to college, and I remember walking by two or three guys who were sweeping the road off William Street in Limerick. I remember as I walked by, one of them looked up and said, "Well done at the weekend Wardy."

'I stopped and had a chat with them, but I just couldn't believe that after only one game these guys on the street knew who I was and the parts of my game that went good or bad.

'Coming from Dublin, rugby was an upper class game played by people who went to the better schools, and certainly as I was involved in soccer as well, very few of the people I played soccer with knew anything about rugby, so that was the way it was in Dublin at the time. There was also the GAA divide, the Northside versus the Southside; rugby went south, and well, Croker is on the north side of the city.

'Limerick crosses all those barriers; there are simply no divides. It's the way the game has been for the last 100 years and it is what has made the game so very special.'

And what is the big difference between Munster and Leinster fans? I mean, it is not as if there are many places more socially diverse than Dublin, and Leinster is one of the most competitive provinces when it comes to the GAA. They have one of the best backlines in world rugby and their fans have a lot to be cheerful about, yet they don't have what Munster have.

According to George Hook it is something more than just the will to support a team or a devotion to the game of rugby.

'If you turn around and you say that all the strengths in Munster are the crowd and tradition and grounds, then these are the things that are strangely absent in Leinster. Leinster has none of that tapestry of history.

'People who watch Munster in Thomond or Musgrave Park are there at almost every opportunity. This wouldn't translate the same with Leinster supporters. They just wouldn't go to the same amount of games. That is the fundamental difference between these great rivals, and in truth, everything that Munster is, Leinster is not.

'The other thing is that over the last five years Munster tended to win while no other team, including Leinster and Ulster, managed to win with the same consistency. People always like to follow a winning team. It is at times as simple as that. I mean, Ireland play seven, eight matches a year, while Munster play every week.

'What kind of people support the English soccer team, and what kind of people support Manchester United, Liverpool and Chelsea? It is the same thing in rugby. Munster is now a club, and it is much easier to identify with Munster as a club than it is with the Irish team, strangely enough. I think that is fairly common to ask for tickets to go to a Munster game rather than an international. I mean, it is more fun, they play more often, there is a greater chance of them winning, and just the romance of getting on a charter flight early in the morning and flying to Toulouse or Bordeaux or Leicester is really special. It's just not the same when you go packing your hip flask and your blanket and heading off to Twickers.

'That's what Munster gave back to their loyal fans; the romance and that sort of feeling of an expedition—something you don't get following the national team.'

Another man who is forced to agree with this condemnation of the Eastern province is Dubliner and Munster convert, Derek Foley. The *Star*'s chief rugby correspondent has managed to form an incredible bond with the fans and players and become by default an honourary Munster man, although his job negates any such bias.

'Leinster's marketing has fallen flat on its face as they are able to market Friday night home games to stockbrokers and media people and their girlfriends,' slams Foley. 'I mean, are you going to tell me that somebody in Meath or Westmeath can name more than one Leinster player?

'I don't see them travelling down in droves from Louth and Athlone to support the boys in Donnybrook. But the Munster thing has been stoked and worked on by the entire province. And in truth, Munster are a far more catholic sporting population, and I mean catholic with a small 'c', than any of the other provinces.

'If you were from Limerick, then you were from a hurling county, a rugby county and, when Limerick City won the league, a soccer county. And in one year Cork won the Eircom league, the hurling All Ireland and Cork Constitution won the AIL. So by definition you have this far more ecumenical operation working in Munster, and not only do they play for the clubs in the province, but in a way they feel like they belong to it, and own a small part of Munster.'

This would match one topic that comes up time and time again when you talk to players or ex-players or coaches; the importance of the red army of fans. And in many ways they become the biggest reason, ahead of glory and honour—winning becomes the payback for turning up.

According to Mick Galwey, they became so important to him that they were almost part of the team talk.

'You do it for the supporters; they are incredible. You can see them, hear them, and feel them when you out there,' he recalled. 'That's one of the special things about Thomond Park; a ticket is like gold dust. Giving a ticket to someone is huge, and when you see what it means to supporters when you meet them after getting into the ground, you understand why 10,000 fans spend all their money getting down to the south of France.'

When I spoke to him he was enthused to get across the idea of the importance of the fans, to him something even more remarkable because at the time of our interview, Munster had yet to climb the dizzy heights of that ultimate success.

'I don't think you have ever watched a rugby match until you have been to watch Munster play a Heineken Cup game at Thomond Park. It is unique, and the fans are loyal. They keep turning up and following the team even though we haven't won it yet. It's a known fact that Munster people don't go on holidays anymore; they go to Munster matches.

'They save up their money and they miss out on their family holidays or their sun holidays and they go to support Munster— which speaks volumes in itself.'

It must also be said that the Munster phenomenon is contagious, and the infection is constantly being spread from within to the four corners of the country. The amount of Munster jerseys that walk down Patrick Street in Cork, or O'Connell Street in Limerick, is now matched by that of Grafton Street in Dublin. The mighty men of Munster have managed to convert rugby fans nationwide, quicker than St Patrick in a pagan village.

For some people it is the excitement of the game or the sense of community, but for all it is a decision made after time spent with friends, drinking and sharing the weirdest of situations, and watching 15 men display the characteristics and virtues that all aspire to but few manage to exhibit. Seeing as I am also a fan, I felt it was necessary to put the voice of a true Munster supporter in the book, and what better than that of a converted Leinster man?

Briain Colgan is a devoted Munster fan who travelled to all the away games, as well as never missing a home game. What separates him from other Limerick, Cork and Tipperary fans is that Briain is from Edenderry in Offaly. Not only is he from Leinster but he currently lives in Sandymount village, in the heart of Dublin 4. So I let him explain what it was that drove him away from the blue of Leinster, his birthright club, and into the bosom of Munster.

'My friend from Offaly, Joe O'Connell, started going to all the Munster matches back in the late 1990s because he was Frankie Sheehan's first cousin and his family are incredibly close to one another, so there was simply no question about it—he is Munster's number one fan.

'Of course Joe needed a travelling buddy, and he of course had to join the Munster Supporters Club, and you were getting the two tickets to go to the games, so when nobody else would go I got the call and that was how a BIFFO (Big Ignorant 'Fecker' from Offaly) became a devout Munster fan.

'From then on we started going to all the away games we could get to, and it didn't matter at all where it was or who it was against. Joe just booked the tickets and I would turn up. We travelled to the

Gloucester away game in 2004 and it was there that I got my first real insight into the mind of the Munster supporters.

'The family aspect was what hit me the most, because even though we weren't from Munster, we were accepted as supporters straight away, and there was no weirdness, no snide comments, just the red of Munster and the hand was shook, and they would just laugh when they found out you were from Edenderry, and in truth were just thrilled that you had made the journey.

'It was never a case of, "What the fuck are you doing here?" or "Fuck off back to Leinster," you were another voice to add to the family, and that was good enough for them and an incredible feeling for me. Joe of course had the family connection, so was an honourary member from the start, but it didn't take long for me to be join up to the Red Army. The next game I went to was in Thomond Park. It was the miracle Gloucester match, and let me tell you, it was there that I learned what real support was.

'There I saw the X-factor; that incredible essence of Munster that all the journalists write about, but you can never fully appreciate it unless you experience it first hand for yourself.'

Of course, for Briain the X-factor was more than just noise and volume, it was also the colour which, when combined with all the other elements, made for an unforgettable experience.

'The other main thing you notice is the red jersey factor; everybody salutes you when you are in the Munster jersey and says hello to you. There is no ignorance or standoffishness with anyone who is representing the red of Munster, and that is special, and you just don't get that with the Leinster crew. At times they barely seem to say hello to each other. I've been to many international and Leinster games, and fans will be fans, but Munster supporters with that red jersey on are something special.

'I was simply blown away by it, it was amazing. The next thing was, I met Frankie Sheehan and his family and his extended player's family, and before long the other players' families, and that was when we became known as the BIFFOs.

'How could you not love it? I mean, you just take that Gloucester away game—there must have only been 2,000 travelling supporters from Munster, but there was an incredible buzz. Kingsholm is a little Thomond Park in England, and you will never shout their fans down, but we gave as good as we got and we all kind of bonded a bit through that.

'You would see the same guys turning up at all the matches and because of this you began to know the heads at the games and you always expected to meet them there the whole time. And sure you would probably end up drinking out of an ice bucket in the arse end of France together, so even the supporters had a sense of community and something in common.

'Not one of them has ever turned around to us converts and said, "That ticket should have gone to a real Munster supporter." And after wearing that Munster jersey to this year's Heineken Cup semi-final against Leinster, which may have been a bit of a betrayal, I will never change back.'

For Briain it was clearly the attitude of the Leinster fans that helped him finally turn his back on Leinster rugby as a true supporter.

'You had every Leinster person who knew you saying, "What the hell are you doing?" and wondering how you could wear such a thing on your back. And of course this was coming from the lads in the pink Ralph Lauren disco shirts who would fork out 300 for a shirt but couldn't be arsed wearing the Leinster jersey. The crowed barely got going for that game and if you started singing or cursing you were told to stop because there were kids present.'

It was all true. It was the Ross O'Carroll-Kelly brigade with the pink shirt, the jumper tied in a knot over the shoulders and the sun glasses on top of the head who were crowded into the North Terrace that sunny day. Briain went on:

'If these guys weren't going to wear jerseys and support their team, then I certainly wasn't going to change my mind and come back to Leinster; in a way it is sad and a little pathetic. I mean, come on lads, you are either supporting a team or you are not, and clearly at times Leinster is without any real supporters and that is a factor as to why they don't really look like winning anything major.'

Throughout the match they were under siege from the Munster supporters, who were chanting and carrying their players to victory. The scenes of Leinster fans silent and leaving the grounds early hit the big screens and told a story of their own.

'You just wouldn't get that sort of blasé attitude with Munster fans. It wouldn't be tolerated for a start. You would be found out early enough, slapped, and sent home to find a jersey and think about what you had done. Munster people don't just have one jersey, they have two or three, and some people get special ones made up for each individual game.

'We had a set made up once and thought we were the bees knees until we left the hotel and realised that half of Munster do that anyway. And some of them were brilliant and witty. You've seen them around the place on banners, like, *'tis your field bull but leave the tinker's daughter alone.*

One t-shirt in particular had '20 Facts you never knew about Paul O'Connell,' which had been adapted from an e-mail circulated around the globe (with various different names at different stages but which never suited anyone as much as the colossal Munster man-mountain):

1. Paul O'Connell has only been scared once in his life and that was the first time he looked in the mirror.

2. Paul O'Connell has counted to infinity; twice.

3. Paul O'Connell does not have ginger hair. It is actually fire, forged from the flames of Mount Doom.

4. The Munster second row does not sleep, he waits.

5. Contrary to popular belief, Paul O'Connell does not have hair on his body because it will not grow on steel.

6. Paul O'Connell is never late. Time slows down to accommodate him.

7. Superman owns a pair of Paul O'Connell Y-fronts.

8. The only thing we have to fear is fear itself …the only thing fear has to fear is Paul O'Connell.

9. Paul O'Connell won't send e-mails. It is faster for him to run.

10. Paul O'Connell ends every relationship with 'It's not me, it's you'.

11. Paul O'Connell is allowed to talk about fight club.

12. He only has one hand. The upper hand.

13. When Paul O'Connell does a push up he isn't lifting himself up; he is pushing the world down.

14. Paul O'Connell can believe it is not butter.

15. The only way Rome was built in a day was if Paul O'Connell ran a construction company.

16. Paul O'Connell once ordered a Big Mac in Burger King. And got it.

17. O'Connell was offered the lead role in Rocky VI but turned it down because he doesn't do children's films.

18. The closest Iraq came to owning weapons of mass destruction was when Paul O'Connell and the Munster team went to Dubai.

19. Paul O'Connell could touch MC Hammer. He just chooses not to.

20. Everybody loves Raymond. Except Paul O'Connell.

'Everywhere you went, there were t-shirts and jerseys like this and everyone was up for the craic, a far cry from what you would find in Dublin 4, for or after a Leinster game. Don't get me wrong, I have followed Leinster as best I could, but the constant disappointments, and I have to say the annoying Ross O'Carroll-Kelly type fans just put me off for life, and Munster has given me a good home thanks to Joe O'Connell.'

Of course Munster matches and fans tended to leave you with more than just the win and the bonus point. More often than not the banter and craic led to situations that became, over time, legends of the Munster Supporters Club.

Briain has more than a few of them but one in particular sticks out in his mind.

'Over at the Gloucester match we got a little too drunk of course, and somehow managed to blag our way into the dressing rooms. We stood outside the tunnel and the dressing rooms were right outside them, and we were tanked up; a girl had been walking around with a five gallon drum of Heineken strapped to her back, and Joe had literally made her part of the group and wouldn't let her leave.

'As a result we kept buying Heineken all through the game and were well on by the end of it, and yet in flying form, even though we lost. So we had positioned ourselves outside the tunnel waiting for the players to come out, just to have a look at them, and Joe just said, "Fuck this!" and pulled out a disposable camera that he had in his pocket.

'He flashed this camera at the security guard at the door and said, "Irish Press," and then the bewildered security guard let him in. The bouncer inside presumed that we had been let in legitimately for some reason, and didn't kick us out. It was unbelievable. So we were standing in the middle of a tunnel and the dressing rooms were to our left and the showers were to our right, and going across the tunnel were all the players, stripped, just wearing towels.

'Suddenly Joe starts running up to all the players as they are going in or coming out and getting them to pose for photographs with his little pocket camera. At that moment the English and Gloucester prop Phil Vicary comes out of the shower and Joe grabs him, throws me the camera, and manages to get him in a head lock for a picture.

'By now the security guards began to wonder what was going on and if these two Irish guys running around with a throwaway camera were really from the press. But it was probably when Joe tossed him the camera and asked him to take a snap of the pair of us with Vicary that the head bouncer came down and put a stop to the mayhem.

'They pegged us out so we took off and headed up towards the bar. In Kingsholm they have a main bar and a member's bar and as we go up to the bar, Joe suddenly disappears, and I meet up with these two other guys and go for a drink in the packed bar. It was so packed that we were really being bet around the place, when suddenly there is this loud tapping on the glass partition that separates the member's bar from the commoner's bar and there is no other than Joe O'Connell, with his face pressed against the glass, and standing behind him is half the Munster team.

'He was waving us in, but after the tunnel incident, the press argument was a no go and we just couldn't get in, but Joe stayed there, happy as Larry, for half the night and eventually managed to sneak us in. Of course by now Joe didn't want to leave, and we were staying in Cardiff, which was about £80 in a taxi ride away. We just about managed to get to Cardiff with him, but we don't know if he ever managed to make it home from there. I mean he was completely clueless.

'It's now a running joke amongst the lads that maybe he never made it home, and that we will probably meet this bearded homeless ex-taxi driver wandering the streets of Cardiff begging for a lift back to Gloucester.'

It's that sort of craic and messing that is also part of the Munster X-factor, and it's why there is such a universal appeal to be a Munster fan over any of the others. It is probably the reason why every other person supports Munster if they aren't playing themselves, and why devoted fans choose to swap their tickets to internationals in Lansdowne Road in place of Thomond tickets for a Heineken Cup night.

Of course, what does help when you have an incredible bandwagon of support is when the players themselves understand what the supporters do for the team, and what they sacrifice. I would have to admit that the players are very accessible if you want to meet them and chat to them. I'm sure the other teams are accessible too, but the Munster players always have time for you, for a little chat that can make you or your kids or anybody there feel that bit special, even for just an hour or so.

If you walk into any of the bars under Thomond Park and stand there for long enough you will meet the players floating about having a chat, and how they put up with it I'll never know, having the backs slapped off them by over-enthusiastic supporters, and being hugged and kissed by anyone and everyone. They must have an amazing tolerance, but I suppose it pays on the big occasions when the support turns up.

Briain is not unaware of the financial pinch that comes with supporting Munster. They are not a cheap team to follow by any standard.

'It's e800-1000 a game without a shadow of a doubt, and in fairness, for every match you may as well write off a grand straight away. That's the only catch, and when you think about it, how they get 3,000 people flying out for all these away games at e1,000 a pop, something special must be going on.

'That's e3,000,000 per game, which is a lot of money by anybody's standards, and then you look at the 60,000 or so fans that walked, ran, flew and swam over to Cardiff this year to be part of the final. How much was spent on that?

'I'd say the sales of fake tan will go through the roof this summer in Limerick and Cork, as there won't be any money left in the bank for a sun holiday after that weekend. It's astonishing, and as I said before, you see the same faces at these matches, so in general it isn't a random 3,000 people travelling, and they are shelling out this cash on a weekly basis at times. Either they are considerably wealthy or incredibly devoted.

'The home matches are always sold out, and even if you do the head count there will always be at least 100,000 people at one of the big miracle matches. And the final; the final is something that I will cherish for the rest of my life.

'In fact what you had over there was thousands of soldiers in the Red Army, queuing up, waiting for battle, getting more and drunk as the afternoon went on, and incredibly out of it all there came a moment of brilliance; an epiphany that stemmed the bleak and bleary morning pints sessions. They were selling match programmes outside the ground so myself and a few others bought them, found a post office and put them in an envelope and posted them home. I believed they were going to win and that I would never hang on to a programme, so I sent one home and it was waiting for me when I got back.'

Munster has given Briain and his friend Joe a rugby identity that they couldn't find in Offaly. They have become part of a phenomenon that is an equal opportunities employer that doesn't discriminate.

The fans are the core, the beating heart of the Munster phenomenon, and with this voice, ethos and attitude; I wouldn't be very surprised if the Munster bandwagon was actually only starting to move.

Imagine what will happen when they get into full swing

MUNSTER RUGBY FACT:

Ian Dowling

While many of the Munster team are seasoned professionals, Kilkenny man Ian Dowling is something of a newcomer. He played six times for Munster in the Heineken Cup and managed to lift the trophy on his first attempt. Hard to believe he was still playing club rugby in the AIL only last year.

'There are no stars in Munster, it's just honesty
and work rate.'
– Jerry Flannery

Chapter 9: What it takes to make the grade

I don't know of any rugby player in any province or country who doesn't strive to play at the pinnacle of the sport. The thought of running out onto the pitch at Lansdowne Road in a Six Nations tie against England is the reason why we rugby players enter the sport and continue, battered and bruised, in the hope of progressing to the highest level.

Certainly, when I played the game at a semi-serious level, I always dreamed of togging out in the brown, wooden-panelled dressing rooms beneath the Lansdowne Road stadium and donning the green jersey of Ireland. That romantic image of myself, standing side by side on the red carpet with the team, while the President of Ireland is being led down the row, the crowd chanting 'Ireland's Call', is something that pushed and drove me through the early years of my sporting career.

But one thing I have learned while writing this book is that at some point in a rugby player's life he is faced with the decision of where to go next with his 'sporting career'. And in the days with limited professionalism or subsidised amateurism, whatever you want to call it, that choice used to be an awful lot harder than it is today.

To put your life on hold for a dream that will more often than not fail to come to true fruition, for no monetary benefit, is a big sacrifice. And at 18, like many other youngsters playing provincial rugby, I decided against the dedicated summer IRFU training camps and opted for the easy life of AIL rugby and an exciting social life. However, in recent years other factors have influenced the growth and career paths of rugby players.

The success of the provincial teams and in particular Munster has offered a more gratifying route to success and international rugby standard. Before the Heineken Cup, a player had to excel, and in many cases leave the country and achieve success in the English Premiership before he was noticed by international scouts, if he wasn't already in the gaze of the international selectors. This meant a huge commitment and lifestyle change that led to players leaving family and friends in pursuit of the ultimate goal.

On the other hand, some promising players were faced with a similar choice and opted to play socially rather than slog it out in the leagues, dreaming of a goal that grew more and more unlikely the longer they played. As a result, many players were lost from the fold, choosing a different path as the route looked harder than it should be. Today that has all changed.

The success of the provincial squads has meant that the successful players are kept at home and are set up with development contracts in their respective areas. In this environment, financial strains are eliminated as they are groomed for the next level, which may be Heineken Cup or Celtic League, but also a route which offers a different path to international places.

The IRFU certainly must be commended for this because the direct result is a greater player pool for both the provinces and international side to pluck from. Another example of their commitment to the development of the domestic rugby player is the establishment of the international club side earlier this year.

Here the finest amateur players perhaps on the brink of a provincial contract or on the way back from the fold can experience an international test match in Lansdowne Road or Twickenham, and thus increase their appetite for the next level. The immediate effect of these measures has been an increase in the draw of the game in this country.

People with promise, who may have been latecomers to the sport, have been given specialist coaching to bring them up to the respective level, and talent that before would have gone unharvested is now making its way up the rugby ladder. One clear example of this lies in the tale of Trevor Hogan, one of the brightest talents this country has seen in the second row.

At the age of 26, he has already gained underage international caps and played in both the Heineken Cup and the Celtic League. He did not attend a recognised rugby playing school and only took up the game very late in life. In a different era he may never have reached the rugby heights he now enjoys. I asked him to explain his late entrance into the rugby fold when I met him preparing for the big match against Perpignan in the Cup earlier this year.

'I didn't start playing rugby until I was about 16 and I was picked up by Nenagh Ormond,' he replied. 'Honestly, I had pretty much been playing soccer and hadn't given rugby a second glance.

'First, I suppose, I managed to play a season at Under 16 and from there I managed to make an Irish development squad, which was brilliant. From there I started to learn and develop all the skills that all the other guys had developed. It was tough but intensive, and I really learned a lot.'

It was here that Hogan was spotted by the Munster set up. Thanks to the reforms in the development system, Trevor was allowed to make up for lost time and his work rate and commitment made him a key acquisition for the branch. And being from Tipperary, he was only too delighted to accept the offer to play his ball in Thomond Park, a dream of his.

'Four years ago I landed a Munster contract and that was like a dream come true, it really was. I think that this was the point where I realised that I could make a living out of the game rather than just playing it as a pastime or as a semi-pro.

'In the long run I suppose people have this sort of opinion that it is an easy living and that it is a bit of a doss but I can tell you now, that simply isn't true. Granted, it might seem like there is a lot more free time than what you would get with a regular nine to five job, but that is only on the surface and in reality that down time is for rest and is actually part of the training.'

And this is where the real value of the IRFU initiative came in. It takes a lot of time and patience for players to adapt to the professional lifestyle and is not something that happens over night. In fact, in many other professions, bosses couldn't afford to give a lengthy period of grace for employees struggling to adjust to a new job. But professional rugby is not like any other job and the physical demands must first be confronted, along with a few more important elements of your personal life.

'It takes a lot of time for yourself and your body to realise that just because you have time off you aren't free and you have to take a rest period seriously. God, it took a while before my girlfriend realised that as well, but sure that is a different story.

Munster Number Eight Denis Leamy contests a split restart as Flannery watches for the tap back.

Taking to the field at Thomond Park before the match against Stade Français, the team could feel the surge of energy and power the '16th man' of the unrivalled home support gave them as they prepared to do battle with the French giants.

Rob Henderson, back in training for Munster, faced a constant fitness battle in the '06 season.

A man apart—Paul O'Connell takes the ball
unchallenged from the night sky at Thomond.
Would you want to try to stop him?

Anthony Foley makes a charge against the Newport Gwent Dragons at Thomond Park.

Marcus Horan celebrates a cheeky try against
Stade Français.

John Kelly flies past the Treviso tight head prop as
Ronan O'Gara follows up in support.

Tempers frayed against Castres in 2002 as tensions mounted and scores were settled; Munster getting revenge for their group defeat by overturning the French side in the semi final.

Another Munster attack is halted when Rob Henderson is caught by the collar against Benneton Treviso.

Fans young and old were out in force to celebrate a proud day in Munster sporting history.

Alan Quinlan shows a clean pair of heels and a safe pair of hands to claim a lineout ball against Gloucester in the 'Miracle Match' of 2003.

Supporting Munster, even when you are from
Offaly, has become a fashionable hobby.

Thousands braved the rain and wind to gather on O'Connell Street in Limerick
to welcome home their team in their hour of triumph and to catch a glimpse of
that Holy Grail; the Heineken European Cup.

Peter Stringer raises the long-awaited prize, the Heineken Cup, before a
huge crowd of ecstatic Munster fans on the team's return home.

Photo © Press 22

The Red Army banners were visible wherever
Munster went, more often than not
outnumbering the opposition's fans in their own
stadiums, and at Fortress Thomond drowning out
all other voices with a cacophony of chants and
roars of encouragement.

Photo © Press 22

'It's not just that though. The nutrition and diet is an extra part that maybe other people with regular jobs don't have to deal with, but it is a key part of my job. Take a typical day's training for a Heineken Cup week like this week against Perpignan. We meet in the gym at 9am for some weight and power training which goes on for an hour and a half. This is fairly serious and heavy work and takes it out of you. Then you break and come back after lunch for some skill and speed training with the coaches on the pitch. Yeah, we are fit enough but it does take its toll on you, especially when the weather isn't the best, and this is Ireland so that is a regular occurrence.'

Another element that enters the mix of the professional rugby player is that of flexibility. With provincial set ups based over the 32 counties, players are scattered all over the country, based in different camps within their relative camps. Before the construction of these specific academies and the advent of professional playing contracts, the four teams were in many ways at the mercy of the players' jobs.

The time training needed to prepare for an interprovincial season, let alone a successful Heineken Cup campaign, was a huge demand and unwavering commitment for those holding down a separate job. The possibilities of players completing a full day's session and then driving 100 kilometres to hook up with the rest of the squad would not only be unlikely but unfair to the members in question.

Now however, working weeks are constructed around a fair and well timetabled set up that is designed to maximise the training schedules of the entire squad and allows for comprehensive sessions. And if the management need to extend training to allow for a bit of essential team work, then over-time is not a problem.

'Later on in the week of the quarter-final, on one particular evening, the Cork boys came up around 7pm to do some specialised lineout work. And you see, that is the other aspect of the Munster squad that you wouldn't get with the other provinces—it is split in two. The Cork boys do their main part of the training in the Cork centre while we go to the University of Limerick for ours.'

As was seen by the Lion's Diary, which documented the progress of the Lion's ill-fated tour of New Zealand, professional rugby has left no stone unturned when it comes to analysing the opponents. This mantra has been adopted by the provincial set ups and all of the Zurich Premiership teams across the water in England.

Something like video analysis, which may have been seen as excessive several years ago, is now commonplace, and in most quarters essential, especially when it comes to the specialist and tactical areas of the opposition. In particular, the emergence of the lineout as a key point of attack and defence has meant that many teams will spend hours watching video footage of an opponent's lineout in the hope of preparing an effective defensive pattern or in the hope of composing a new move to expose a tiny weakness. For Munster in the Heineken Cup this was a regular occurrence for the players involved.

Hogan told me: 'Perpignan had a really organised lineout, both in attack and defence, so we had to meet up to devise a strategy to defend it. That comes from another aspect of the modern professional era—video analysis. We spend hours viewing tapes of our next opponents, working out how we are going to play them. Figuring out their strengths and their weaknesses so that we can exploit them when the time comes around is now a major part of our pre-match sessions.

'All of this and the extra training mean we have to stay late and makes one of the longer days, but once again they have to be done on any Heineken Cup week. That day the Cork boys came up we didn't get home until well after 9pm, but sure there was still time for a cup of tea and "Podge and Rodge" so there were no complaints.'

Thank heaven for small mercies. Trevor concedes that at times they are the main talking point for the entire squad. And in this way professional rugby draws parallels with most other jobs, with "Podge and Rodge" forming the basis of their water cooler conversation.

It may be a physical position where bonuses are based on wins and yards gained rather than targets, but the players certainly appear to have moved on from the pay for play ethos of the early 1990s.

'I'd be lying if I said it wasn't an enjoyable job but there definitely is a perception out there that it is a walk in the park when it isn't. As one of the younger squad members, there is an intense feeling of pride and ambition to get on the first team and play for the province. Personally, I had a taste of the Heineken Cup last year and now all I want to do is get back onto the first team to get more of that action.'

As has happened so often during the research and interviews for this book, the mention of the Munster jersey evokes the same emotion time and time again—pride.

And Trevor is no different. His late blossoming and tardy arrival to the peaks of the profession have only whetted his appetite for the red jersey of the new European champions.

'There really is something special about playing for Munster and it is something I learned late in life as I started playing rugby so late in my career. It is pride and it is regularly said in the dressing room that you know you are not just wearing that jersey for yourself but you are representing your family, friends, province and everyone who has gone before you wearing that jersey.'

But with that jersey comes a great responsibility that all of the players accept and deal with on a daily basis. The history and the great players of the past act as a spiritual connection between past and present, victories and failures.

With this great responsibility comes an element of respect and even a sense of fear that can have a positive or negative effect on the current crop of rising stars.

'Sometimes I think it is fear itself that motivates me and the fear of letting my friends and family down as well as my team mates,' said the 6ft 5 Shannon second-rower. 'But there definitely is something special with Munster over the other three provinces and that gives you that extra edge to want to succeed with them. I think it is most evident around the week of a Heineken Cup game. There is just something so special about a Heineken Cup game that is not there any other time.'

Trevor is somewhat philosophical when it comes to Munster's reputation and at times their failure to rise to the occasion when they play in a lesser competition. But he is also optimistic and refreshingly honest when it comes to fixing the problem in the hope that Munster can become the supreme European team in the near future.

'I know it is something that we try to replicate for the Celtic League and Cup but it just doesn't seem to work out. It is hard to describe but there is just a different feeling about the team and the training sessions that week and Jerry (Flannery) and Pete (Stringer) would all tell you the same thing. It is just a different buzz.

'You would be walking down the street, and granted, people might not recognise me that often, but when they do they are wishing me well and shaking my hand and it is just great. Then, depending on the game, you could be running out onto the pitch in front of a packed Thomond Park crowd, playing for points in a vital crunch game. And that is what sport is about and what Munster is all about.

'I don't know; it is probably something you get when you play for any team where your friends are involved, but with the Munster team there is also a great sense of history and pride. Like, how many players would have joined a team only to be training and playing beside Mick Galwey and Jim Williams? I mean, for someone who blossomed at this game late in life you couldn't pick two better guys to help you with your game, and of course that only increases your desire to play for the first team.

'I consider myself lucky in a way to be playing here, but as you say, I am on the periphery of the team and my goal like any of the other younger players is to break into the first team, get a regular spot and play in more of those important home games. Of course it is easy to get hung up on Munster's special relationship with the Heineken Cup and the, "will they won't they" argument.'

Thankfully that pressure has now been eliminated by the titanic campaign the boys in red unleashed on Europe this past season. But Trevor, like many of the players and pundits, is not sure what will happen next. Now that romantic journey has reached the holy shores and plucked the grail from the hands of the French maiden in Biarritz, will they just be satisfied with the one win or will this be the start of a major assault on Europe?

'Personally I think it is only a matter of time before we win the Cup, but I wonder what will happen then,' revealed the Tipperary

133

man. 'I mean, when you have won it once, where do you take it from there? I mean, will pundits and journalists be demanding that we regain it next year and then go for three in a row?

'Like, before we may not have won it but we had played some great games and provided the supporters with some great games along the way. In the end they are what really matter to this Munster team. You can only really experience what a difference the crowd make when you are playing.

'It was truly mind blowing to be there for the Sale game or the Gloucester game, where the crowd just changed things and I don't think either team were ever in with a chance. For these reasons I think the future of Munster is safe, and it's why young people like myself go out and train as hard as we do to try and get a regular spot in the team.' Having finally made it to the top, Munster Rugby will no doubt see a long line of young hopefuls setting their sights on that red jersey.

MUNSTER RUGBY FACT:

Playing Away from Home

Just in case Munster feel they have a monopoly on the Heineken Cup, our Celtic cousins Wales also have a special relationship with the competition. All in all, eight Welshmen have picked up coveted winner's medals, without a Welsh team ever having won the Cup. They include Gareth Thomas with Toulouse, lock Tony Rees with Brive, Bath's Ieuan Evans, Richard Webster and Nathan Thomas, Northampton's Alan Bateman and Andy Newman, and of course Robert Howley with London Wasps.

'In sport or in life it is hero one day and zero the next.' – Declan Kidney

Chapter 10: Where it all began

One of the great advantages of history is being able to learn from your mistakes, and certainly for the Munster team this had to be taken into account in order for them to exorcise their demons and at last lift the Heineken Cup.

All the bad calls, learning curves and crooked lineouts, the robbed tries, the lucky bounces, all had to be taken into account before Munster could negotiate their way to this year's final.

Looking back to where the European adventure first really began for the Munster team and it's much coveted (and well trained) Red Army, you have to look at their first win in the competition. It began in Thomond Park, in November 1995, when Munster defeated a much better Swansea team by 17-13; their first European Cup match and their first win. As Mick Galwey admitted to me when I met him, it was probably a game they shouldn't have won on paper but grit, steel and passion carried them through that day.

The local supporters weren't quite sure what to make of this hastily arranged competition, but 2,500 did turn out to see the home side take a step into the unknown—they would go on to multiply like bacteria, desperately seeking success and the ability to eke out tickets where there appeared to be none, in order to colonise an army that would eventually take over Europe.

And while it may have started the European dream for Munster, it also began a bleak and flavourless time for the southern team who lost away game after away game, never really making any sort of an impact on a competition that really began to grow in credibility and importance.

In October 1997, Harlequins narrowly beat a struggling Munster side, 48-40 in what was to be one of the best games of the season. They shared 11 tries in a genuine epic and the sides were locked at 30-30 at one point in the second half. But Munster allowed Keith Wood's side to edge away in the final minutes as they became over anxious, something they would never repeat again when the going got tough.

The real breakthrough for Munster came at Vicarage Road in November 1999, when the Munster rabble defeated the then aristocrats of English and European rugby, Saracens, by a single point in an intense cliff hanger. Munster were 21-9 down at half time and 34-23 down with 10 minutes to go, but a late Jeremy Staunton try and Ronan O'Gara conversion won the day.

From then on Munster began to attack the competition and earn a self-belief and confidence that would bring them down a cruel and frustrating road full of limbo, penance and purgatory. Eventually, with enough lessons learned, they would come out the other side grasping silverware and crowned heroes.

One man who braved the hard yards but missed the glory was former Munster full back and out half Jeremy Staunton. There for the beginning of the journey, two final losses and two semi-final defeats, Staunton departed for Harlequins and then moved to London Wasps before the Holy Grail was finally grabbed.

But Staunton remembers the beginning, and every hard lesson Munster had to take. For him it started in the 1999 campaign that would eventually lead the now kings of Europe to their first major final; only to lose.

'I had a good season with Garryowen the year before so I was straight into the Munster squad that year, and sure everyone thought it would be the same rigmarole—that we would do well at home but that we wouldn't stand a chance in the long run.

'And I suppose in a way we started out by setting our goals like that and for qualifying for the quarter-finals, but we never really dreamt that we would go to the final. In truth, at the beginning of the year our main goal was to win the interprovincial championship, which we did, and we won all six games as well, which set us up well for the campaign.

'My first European cap, which was my second senior Munster cap, was against Pontypridd in Thomond Park and we won that, which was an incredible feeling, and that really started the search for the Heineken Cup. The next game of course was the famous Saracens away miracle match and it also happened to be my first start.

'So there I was starting a game at Vicarage Road and Saracens had any amount of international stars in their team; Francois Pienar, Michael Lynagh; Richard Hill; Thierry La Croix. All I could think at the time was, Jesus Christ, I'm only 18 years old playing against these guys; all the Super 12 stars, you name it.'

Things didn't go well for the men from Munster as the stars, including no less than eight internationals, began to ruck and maul them around the place. From the touchline it looked like it was going to be just another year for Munster, some impressive home form but a lousy record away from Fortress Thomond.

But then something incredible happened, something which many players consider more important than any of the other miracle matches, a catalyst that would spark the flame of one of the most romantic, unrequited love stories since Wuthering Heights.

'I think we found ourselves 20 points down at half-time and in real danger of getting our arses kicked—that fairly brought me down to earth,' laughs Staunton as he remembers the incredible occasion. 'The second half then we just got really stuck into them and clawed our way back. I got a try and Ronan O'Gara kicked the conversion to win it.

'I got a great ball from Mike Mullins who put me over just underneath the post and the celebrations were brilliant, because that was our first really big win away from home, history had been made, and we had really started going.'

But making history was something that Jeremy and Munster got a quick taste for, and their next game was in Stade les Sept Derniers, in December 1999 against Colomiers. Munster had never won on the road against a French team but after their incredible win over star-studded Saracens, things began to go right for the men in red. Colomiers had lost in the final to Ulster the previous year and all indications were that Munster were heading for their fifth straight defeat in France.

But the visitors produced an outstanding display, with Marcus Horan, on his first start in Europe for Munster, scooting in like a centre to score the late try that clinched the game.

'We actually played well and we actually hammered them,' recalls Jeremy. 'It wasn't easy, don't get me wrong, there is no such thing as an easy win in France, but we worked hard at it and got a great try for Marcus who popped up there, and we had created history again.'

From there the momentum really began to take over the team and when the French arrived in Cork, not to provide aid against the English, but to find revenge for the previous week, they were on a hiding to nothing.

'We were playing well and we started getting momentum, and people suddenly began to talk about us, The following week we were playing Colomiers in the return back to back leg in Musgrave Park in Cork, and for the first time in years the ground was full.

'We beat them hands down that day, a typical French side that lost interest with nothing to play for, and we ran away with it in the end. So all of a sudden we had won four from four, had a dream start, and all we needed was one more game to get through to the quarters and achieve our intended goal of the season, which was to qualify out of the group.'

But that wasn't going to be easy. While the French had taken their beating badly, the internationals at Saracens were left with a gaping wound to lick, along with some seriously bruised egos. But incredibly it would be those egos that would inspire the Munster team to victory as some trash talking about Thomond proved another great leveller.

'Next up was the Saracens return game and we had them in Thomond Park, and that was just the best ever. I mean the place was just packed with 18,000 plus. That was when we really started to get exposure on the national stage by the media both at home and abroad. Before, nobody had known anything about us because in fairness we hadn't done much of note. They knew about 'The Claw' Clohessy, 'Gallaimh' and 'Woody' playing but that was really as far as it went.

'The rest of us didn't have international caps, some of us only had a handful of AIL games and were on part-time contracts, just your normal Joe Soap on the street who had suddenly won four from four in the European Cup; it was crazy. They were fairly cocky, they were coming to Thomond Park and trying to teach us a lesson and in the weeks coming up to the game we were reading quotes from Bracken and Pienar saying they are coming over to show us how to really play in Europe.

'I remember thinking, "Are these guys saying this coming to Thomond Park?" We completely took motivation from that and in fairness they were a really class side and really gave it to us in the end. For a while it looked like they could walk the walk and had the game won.'

But they didn't win the game that night and a packed house in Limerick, combined with one of the greatest performances ever to grace Thomond Park, saw Munster put a double over the Londoners. And to add insult to injury it was the prodigal son, Keith Wood, returning for the year, who scored the last minute try before the unerring young buck O'Gara slotted the conversion from the touch line to take the win, leaving Sarries with nothing but some harsh words to eat and an extremely bitter pill to swallow.

'When Woody went in for the try and "ROG" kicked the conversion in off of the post, before Langford blocks down an almost certain drop goal and we won by a point or two—it was game over and the place just erupted.

'Limerick that night was like the first major sporting event since the All Blacks game and people were just having the time of their lives, revelling in the atmosphere. I was a young guy and this was my first season and I had been involved in all the games, so in a way I was a bit shocked, like most of the team, because we had surprised even ourselves and guaranteed ourselves the home quarter-final.

'We were beaten by Pontypridd the following week but with the mental state of the players—we were all shattered—there was no way we could beat them, but we had guaranteed the quarter-final so nobody minded too much.'

From then on, things changed permanently for the Munster team. As they broke for the Six Nations campaign, it was the men from the south who stole the column inches, spotlights and radio interviews. Everybody wanted to be a part of the Munster journey. They were the great white hope of Irish Rugby and there wasn't a rugby fan alive who didn't want to latch onto the rolling bandwagon.

'Every day we just got more and more exposure; players doing interviews; people queuing for tickets; and even people watching us train. We weren't really used to this and it seemed to be just crazy, but I suppose the phenomenon of Munster Rugby that has surrounded us had arrived. When you play for Munster you never really separate yourself from the supporters and the hype because they are part of it as well. And I suppose nobody really knew what was happening at the time and even the lads today will tell you that those experiences stood to them in the third final—how to deal with the pressure and the hype was something that took years to master.

'Did we get caught up in the past? I don't know, maybe some players did. I was just young enough to just get on with things but Declan Kidney was always trying to make us aware and not to get too caught up in the hype. He would remind us that we had fought hard to get there and in one game it could be all over. In sport or in life it is hero one day and zero the next, and that was something he always said.'

When it came down to the home quarter-final the Munster bandwagon really began to roll. In what was to be one of the performances of the tournament, Munster beat Stade Français 27-10 in a try-scoring exhibition against the French. When the semi-finals came, Munster couldn't believe their bad luck when out of the pot came the masters of French rugby, Toulouse, away from the Limerick fortress, in Bordeaux.

Against all the odds and with an incredible travelling support, Munster lined out as complete underdogs to face Toulouse in their first semi-final. Once again they revelled in the underdog mantle and from the first whistle, in the extreme heat, they tore into the much-fancied French side. Tries from John Hayes of all people, O'Gara, and Jason Holland were just too much as they overpowered the stunned French operatives. Three tries to one and a cheeky score line of 31-25 to the men in red saw them march on to their first European Cup final.

So, roll on the final in Twickenham in May 2000 and a Munster carnival atmosphere, with many of the fans celebrating the job before it had been done. For the first time in their European history Munster were favourites, a tag it seems that Munster would never learn to cope with. With one minute of the final to go and Munster just one point down, Ronan O'Gara watched as his penalty headed towards the target before just veering wide of the left hand post. As the touch judge's flags lulled in the breeze, the arms stayed down and as the ball fell to earth with a thud, so did the realisation that Munster had lost. A heartbreaking defeat it was but one that only renewed Munster's European attitude.

The final scoreboard that day read a resounding Northampton 9-Munster 8. The Cup would find a home at Franklin's Garden's, while Munster would have to pick themselves up and lick their wounds.

'Well when you look at it, it was probably the best chance we had of winning it, on paper anyway,' recalled Staunton. 'People are always going to say, you know, that the first one is the one to win, and we were the better team, but maybe we did get caught up in our own emotion and left it all behind us.

'I always felt we had a better team than Northampton but maybe they were better prepared and just had to win. They didn't have the hype or the support that we had. Sometimes that great support can be a negative when it turns into pressure and expectation, and we probably weren't best equipped to deal with it on the day and just got really, really nervous.

'We knew ourselves in the dressing room afterwards that we would be back here again though, and that something special had started. Declan and Brian O'Brian and "Gallaimh" were going around to us saying, "We have the belief now, we know we can do it." Before that competition, psychologically we always thought that French and Premiership teams were better than us, because we were only the Irish Paddies and they were the cream of the professional ranks in the UK and Europe, playing for England and France.

'In the past I suppose we always thought, fair enough, we will try our best but in the end probably take a beating from them, but that year we said, right, we are fucking better or as good as them and we have every right to win this cup just as much as they do.

'I remember before the first pre-season game the following season, "The Claw" telling us all it was like riding a bike and that you just have to get back on it and go again, and that is exactly what we did.

'We were unlucky then the following year, losing out to Stade Français in the semi-final, because we had all believed that we would play better and it would not be just our support that would get us through, and with the confidence we were building we could turn up as favourites and have nothing to fear. But on the day that second year, John O'Neill's try that was disallowed began to put questions into people's minds and they began to question whether we would ever win the damn thing or not.

'Whenever it seemed that things were going our way, or when it looked like we were destined to win it, something tragic turned up and our dream was taken away from us, and maybe we were beginning to learn a lesson that you had to lose one or two before you can win it.'

But year in year out the Munster Machine would turn up at the start of the season, safe in the knowledge that this year would be their year. 2002 looked as good as any for the Kidney crew, as they powered their way into an away quarter-final against old rivals Stade Français. It was a game they would win away from home by the margin of a lowly conversion, 14-16 to the Munster men. But again an unfortunate draw gave them a semi-final away from home against old rivals Castres Olympiques, another titanic French side.

Once again the troops rallied and in a remarkable exhibition of devotion, the Munster faithful almost turned Castres into a home game, singing, chanting and probably boozing their way into the ascendancy. That day, as if inspired by the fans, Ronan O'Gara scored a decisive try and six penalties, to add to John Kelly's try, to beat Castres 25-17. It was the final once again, three years down the line, and surely this was to be their year. They faced Martin Johnson and his motley crew of Leicester Tigers in the Millennium Stadium in May 2002.

But once more Munster were found wanting, although this time it may not have been their fault. Staunton remembers it well:

'That was probably the hardest route to the final we have ever had and we had played some really tough games and had been denied a home draw. It was a really hard-fought victory against Castres, and we really truly believed that this was going to be it. We were even getting to the stage where it came to a really close game and it was down to the last few minutes and we thought we were going to do it.'

But when it came down to the last few minutes and Munster were 15-9 down with a scrum on the five metre line, the unthinkable happened. *That* incident happened; a bizarre moment in sporting history where one man's actions changed the course of the game for ever.

Neil Back made the headlines for his 'intervention' at a last minute scrum, knocking the ball out of Peter Stringer's hands and costing Munster their last shot at the title. The 'Hand of Back' would take the trophy from the Munster team and place it firmly in the grasp of man-mountain Martin Johnson. Munster were once again left to re-group and try to pull the pieces of what was now looking like a never-ending quest for glory. Despite the injustice though, Staunton remained magnanimous and philosophical in defeat.

'Leicester on the day scored two tries and we didn't score any, and you know, that to me was the difference. People are always going to talk about the 'Hand of Back', and obviously that is just one of those things that would only happen against Munster, but on the day the record will only remember that they lifted the Cup. And to their credit I think Leicester were at the peak of their domestic and European dominance and had some fantastic players.

'Darren Garforth, Martin Johnson, Ben Kay, Neil Back and Martin Corry, on the day they showed their class and managed to clinch their second consecutive title. But it was a heartbreaking, gut-wrenching experience for us and I can remember the dressing room afterwards. Nobody said anything for over half an hour.

'We thought we had done everything in our preparation to win it and there we were, falling at the final fence every time. At that point I think we began to doubt our own belief and our own talent when really we shouldn't have, and it was very hard to pick ourselves up after that. We didn't want to be the bridesmaids, the team who never win anything but are always courageous and gracious losers. We wanted to be ruthless and win it regardless of how we did it or how many people we pissed off.'

The next year would see the departure of long time coach and servant Declan Kidney to the IRFU, and the end of the most successful coaching era in Munster rugby. In his stead came the tried and tested Aussie coach Alan Gaffney. While he would never manage to take the team where Kidney had, to the brink of success only to meet failure, he would introduce the players and Staunton to a different style of coaching. And he would also lead the players where Kidney had previously failed, and win their first piece of major silverware.

'It was a nice change and almost a breath of fresh air for the players, and with no disrespect to Declan, he had been with us for four years now and we came up short in the European Cup twice, and had lost the Celtic League final to Leinster, and were beginning to wonder if we would ever win something.

'Under Gaffney we started really well in the Celtic League and we then went on to win it and it looked like things were beginning to change, like we were learning to cope with the Munster baggage and beginning to win things. And that Celtic League final was on in the Millennium Stadium, and that win helped us erase the memories of the defeat to Leicester.'

What Jeremy fails to include at this point is that a few weeks previously Munster pulled the comeback to beat all comebacks out of the fire against Gloucester in Thomond Park. It was a game in January 2003 that will forever be remembered by all true red fans.

Already much like the All Blacks game, over 100,000 people are claiming to have attended the 13,000 capacity stadium of Thomond where the impossible was achieved by 15 brave soldiers. In a game that finished Munster 33-Gloucester 6, the score line fails to tell the real story.

Thanks to a blundered pool campaign, Munster found themselves staring at the brink of eviction from their beloved Heineken Cup. Nobody could quite believe it, especially the Gloucester team, but strange things happen at Thomond Park. The supporters expected nothing more than to stretch an unbeaten sequence at the ground. The odds against winning a place in the Heineken Cup quarter-finals were huge.

Having to score at least four tries and win by 27 points, against Gloucester, appeared to be just too much to ask. Hailed as the strongest mauling pack in Britain, Gloucester barely got a look in as Munster attacked their line out throws, pulling, grabbing and interfering, while winning their own with considerable ease.

The rolling maul is hard to stop, and Gloucester's, according to some English coaches, is impossible to break down, yet on a night when it seemed that anything was possible, Munster stopped them at source to such effect that they only conceded one penalty in that area of the game.

After O'Gara and Mercier exchanged penalties, John Kelly's opening try on 17 minutes was the product of a perfectly weighted pass from Stringer. It mattered not that Mercier, after Gloucester's one spell of dominance, managed to cut the arrears with his second penalty. Munster took over again and O'Gara kicked his second before Holland's delicate chip through gave Mossie Lawlor the space to get in behind the defence for another try three minutes into injury time. The timing could not have been better and the miracle was on.

Munster started the second-half as they had finished the first—in total control. O'Gara kicked his third penalty and then brilliantly converted Mick O'Driscoll's corner flag try, again after a beautifully judged kick to the corner from Holland. Then came the moment the miracle became the reality.

We will never know what might have been had Mercier elected to kick for goal instead of trying to open up Munster's mean defence late in the game. Munster drove forward and Kelly was sent in for his second try. 86 pulsating minutes after they had been considered beyond hope, Munster had achieved the impossible by putting England's finest to the sword.

'It was a great season up until we lost the semi-final and I was really part of the team, and had started most of the games, and when you put the Gloucester match and winning the Celtic League on top of that, I really began to play well that season,' says Staunton.

'And I am not being cocky here but Thomond Park is a great place to play, and I have played there with Munster and against Munster and it is a fantastic ground. It's not like going to Leicester or Gloucester where it is actually intimidating, because the supporters of Munster really respect the opposition and really get behind the team. They won't boo you or get overly abusive from the touchline, it's just a fantastic atmosphere and they respect the opposition if they put up a fight, and that is what got to Henry Paul and Gloucester that year.

'We went to Leicester away and really hockeyed them, and of course Munster luck being what Munster luck was, we ended up drawing Toulouse away. We were like, for fuck sake, what do we have to do to win this competition? I mean, the effort we were putting in was relentless and it didn't seem to be going anywhere, there was no let up, and we lost to Toulouse by a single point. And of course if you look over the four years that I had played in the tournament, every team that beat us ended up lifting the Cup, which was a real sickening feeling.'

It was the same scenario in April 2004 when a much fancied Munster side got London Wasps in a 'home' semi-final, played in Lansdowne Road. Despite a stirring second-half comeback, which put Munster 10 points up with 10 minutes to go, Wasps fought back in turn and a Trevor Leota try in extra-time left Peter Stringer, Jim Williams, Frankie Sheehan and the rest of the Munster men devastated at the final whistle. The final score was Wasps 37-Munster 32, and it would be two years before Munster would fully recover from that titanic blow.

It was Lansdowne Road, April 2004, Munster 32-Wasps 37, and more heartache for Munster, with Joe Worsley, Ayoola Erinle, Simon Shaw, Lawrence Dallaglio and assorted others celebrating having stuck another dagger in Munster's heart. In August 2004 Staunton left Thomond Park and joined London Harlequins and from there joined London Wasps in 2005.

'It was hard for me to leave without the European title but it was harder for the likes of "The Claw", "Gallaimh" and Cillian Keane.

Those boys gave their hearts and souls for Munster Rugby. I was lucky that I came to Munster at an early age and had a chance to play elsewhere as well, which to be honest was something I was always going to do regardless of whether Munster won or not.

'In today's world rugby is professional and you are judged by how many medals you win. I am only realising now having played for Wasps that it really is all about winning and you want to have a medal in the cabinet for every year you play, and I fell short with Munster on numerous occasions. Yeah, I was fairly gutted to be leaving Munster, that was my own decision, but it did feel like unfinished business, especially losing to Wasps the year I left.

'I was losing faith in the whole thing and I left, and talking to the players after they lost in the quarter-finals to Biarritz, they were getting fed up too. They knew they had the talent and they knew they were a good side, but they were just beginning to doubt themselves that little bit.'

Another bow out in 2005, this time rather fittingly in the quarter-finals to Biarritz, would leave the Munster men with plenty of time to consider the mountain they needed to climb. But then came the return of Declan Kidney to the side, who brought with him some expectation, and as a schoolteacher, a willingness to look at the past for answers to the future.

For Munster a change was definitely as good as a rest, and a fresh approach was taken for their 2006 European assault. For Jeremy however, those Munster days are over, for now, as he sets his sites on capturing a European trophy of his own with London Wasps.

'When I left on my own back I knew they always had it and it was only a matter of time, but I just didn't have that time. I'll never forget the time I played there and the effort I put in almost making it, and I know that the guys today will have taken something from all our hard work in the past.'

And with a host of fit and bright new stars and another miracle in the bag, the 2006 season would make all the difference for the mighty men from Munster.

MUNSTER RUGBY FACT:

The Appeal of the Heineken Cup

For those who doubt the draw of the competition; in the 2005 – 2006 campaign, almost a million fans attended Heineken Cup action, with 660,000 attending pool games alone. This was followed by four sell-out quarter-finals in Ireland, England, France and Spain. The final saw a capacity crowd of over 77,000.

'It's the culmination of seven years work. I wouldn't like to think of the consequences if we'd lost.'
– Shaun Payne

Chapter 11: The road to victory

The rugby season for 2005/2006 certainly did not give the preview of the great things that were hiding around the corner. The national team was struggling during the autumn internationals and a poor performance against the French in Paris gave the impression that the worst was inevitable. And while it has been a long time since the wooden spoon stirred the pints of the Emerald isle, it was looking like Italy were sick of being spanked with it.

Another close *get out of jail free* game in Lansdowne Road was the catalyst or kick in the arse that Ireland needed to light the proverbial fire under them, and like that, rugby came alive in Ireland. Victories against the Welsh and Scottish set up a mouthwatering Triple Crown match against the floundering English team, struggling to emulate their recent successes, and fill the great hole left behind by the departure of Sir Clive Woodward.

The additional carrot in front of the eager horse was that the match was to be played on the Saturday after St Patrick's Day, which also coincided with the completion of the Cheltenham Festival. In essence, what you had was a massive Paddy invasion of

London, and even with a population of over 20 million, everywhere you looked there was a bunch of devoted Irish fans, swamping Guinness and singing of some long lost fields in Galway.

The rugby clubs of London Welsh had adopted their Celtic brethren and under the white canvas of a large marquee the Richmond based club started celebrations and tendered medicinal cocktails for the party-wearied Paddies who graced their doors. The magnitude of the occasion was not lost on the ticket touts who were willing to fork out £1,000 per ticket from anyone who had a less than successful week at the track.

The result was a feverish atmosphere in the hallowed arena of Twickenham, against the World Cup holders, who were still smarting from two successive defeats from their island neighbours. Most talked about the possibility of a damp squib, given the nature of the fixture, but O'Driscoll and his charges were of a different mind. In what would prove to be an incredibly contentious game, Ireland would pip the Brits to sneak the new Triple Crown trophy.

The awesome Shane Horgan sneaked the opening and crucial final try for Ireland, after the English and the boot of Andy Goode looked like they had kicked Ireland back to the nearest London airport, to be escorted home by Michael O'Leary's mob. And as O'Driscoll greedily lifted the shield, Irish rugby's pride was restored and resurrected to the heights that the players richly fought hard for and deserved. It highlighted a never-say-die spirit, and reinforced a mantra and ethos that has seen many Irish teams, in many codes, punch above their weights; anything is possible.

Around the same time, another Irish team was getting ready to prove that miracles not only happen, but are a divine right once the right penance and sacrifices have been paid to the rugby gods. Much like the national team's journey to the top of the mountain, the start of Munster's 2006 Heineken Cup campaign looked ominous.

On 21 October their first outing against Sale away, in a fire-cracker opening to Pool 1 at Edgeley Road, made many neutral fans think twice about booking time off in May, and is probably one of the reasons the bookies would end up shelling out millions to the loyal fans later that year. While many Shark's fans still talk about their skipper Jason Robinson racing 60 metres up the pitch, notching his side's second try and finally condemning mighty Munster to a pointless trip back across the Irish Sea, one name still commands respect in the Munster camp; Sebastien Chabal.

In a virtuoso display of hard hitting and strong running, the French back rower broke the Munster lines time and time again, leaving the men in red seriously wanting. Sale were last season's European Challenge Cup winners and were on a mission to add a second European trophy to their cabinet.

Chabal's dominance aside, the first half was a battle of the boots between old Lion's rivals Charlie Hodgson and Ronan O'Gara. Hodgson's territorial game looked to be giving the Sharks the extra edge, pinning the Irishmen into the corners at every opportunity, but the calmness of O'Gara at crunch times saw Munster lead 10-9 at the break. Three Hodgson penalties accounted for the Sharks' points, while one from O'Gara was followed by a lesson in lineout play from the pack.

With Sale's Argentinean international lock, Ignacio Fernandez Lobbe, in the sin bin, O'Gara nudged the ball into the corner where Frankie Sheen eventually touched down with a ferocious driving maul from the resulting lineout. O'Gara added the conversion.

But even though Munster led at half-time, the Sharks had had the majority of the territory, and the writing all but looked on the wall with the dominance of Chabal and prop Andrew Sheridan, who were making serious inroads into the Munster defence. By the end of the game Chabal had made such an impact he had not only picked up the Heineken Man of the Match award, but he had sent Italian prop Federico Pucciariello back to the 1960s with an incredible tackle that led to Robinson's kick and chase score.

While that try sealed the game, and ensured Munster didn't pick up a bonus point, it was the ten points the home side picked up while Munster hooker Sheehan was in the sin bin after 50 minutes that really turned the fortunes. No sooner had Sheehan departed than the Sharks followed the Munster lead by driving a close range lineout and hunting a try. But somehow the visitors kept them out and then turned the Sharks' scrum to claim their own put in five metres out.

They struck the ball well enough, but Anthony Foley couldn't control at Number 8 and scrum half Tomas O'Leary failed to touch down over his own line, and could only watch in horror as his opposite number, Sililo Martens, followed up to bag a sucker try. Hodgson added the conversion to his earlier penalty and the Sharks were in the driving seat.

As brave as Munster were in defence, they couldn't match the power of Chabal and team in attack, and when Pucciariello lost control of the ball in the tackle inside the Sharks' half, Hodgson kicked long and Robinson easily won the chase for the decisive second try.

The nail in Munster's coffin came from English darling Jason Robinson, but the move summed up the complete performance of a French maestro. As Sale marched on to the possibility of a home quarter-final, the fancied men of Munster were sent back to Limerick to lick their wounds.

From there they prepared to bounce back against the next challenge of the visiting French giants, Castres. Any team who takes a game against Munster in Thomond Park is in for a rude awakening, especially when the Munster team is nursing some pricked pride. And the Thomond Park fortress remained unbreached after Declan Kidney's men sent Castres home to France without a point.

Munster had never lost a Heineken Cup match at Thomond Park, and they weren't about to let that happen when Castres arrived on 29 October, 2005. It was a much-needed victory after a heavy first-round loss to Sale Sharks, and Munster could travel to the struggling Newport Gwent Dragons in December confident of another five points.

Once again it was British and Irish Lions out half Ronan O'Gara who controlled the game beautifully, keeping the French on the back foot with another flawless performance with the boot and hands. The 14 points from his boot kept the home side in front throughout. Fellow Lion Donnacha O'Callaghan was driven over the try line in the opening minutes, and things looked ominous for the visitors.

The visitor's Laurent Marticorena pegged back some lost ground with two penalty goals, but the famous Munster maul was soon in action again as it carried hooker Jerry Flannery over the line for their second try. Winger Anthony Horgan made it three before Castres hit back through impressive out half Romain Teulet, but the French side had the wind at their backs for the first half and they were never going to overturn a 19-13 deficit at the break.

Marticorena and Ronan O'Gara swapped penalties as the weather worsened, and Munster confirmed their bonus point in the 64th minute when winger John Kelly collected a pinpoint O'Gara cross-kick to score. O'Gara converted from the touchline to make it 32-16 and seal the victory. Inside centre Trevor Halstead used his power and pace to add Munster's fifth try, and the home side could even afford to lose winger Shaun Payne to the sin bin without conceding any points. In fact, their defence in the final ten minutes was just as effective as their attack in the first 70 minutes.

Much like the national team, Munster were beginning to get some momentum, and when they went to Wales to slay the Dragons on 10 December, there was only ever going to be one true outcome. They beat them conclusively; 8-24. But it was the reverse fixture a week later in Thomond that would prove most problematic for the Munster European campaign.

That day in Limerick, Newport Gwent Dragons came mightily close to destroying Munster's unbeaten Heineken Cup record at Thomond Park, but ultimately left Ireland without even a losing bonus point, as the home side racked up the points in the final minutes. Paul Turner's Welsh outfit looked a different side, bullying the Munster pack and back line for the majority of the match, and led 17-18 with ten minutes to play.

Munster led 10-8 at half time, but looked to be gaining control when Anthony Foley weaved a bit of magic down the touchline. The back rower who has played more Heineken Cup matches than any other player—an amazing 71—took the ball on the wing, toed ahead and re-gathered for his 21st Heineken Cup try. But Turner, who obviously spotted the chance to upset mighty Munster, sent on Owen and Morgan at half time and they combined for Morgan's touchdown.

O'Gara restored the traditional order of things at Thomond Park with a penalty goal from in front, and made up for several mistakes with a superb 52 metre effort that ricocheted off the left-hand upright and over the bar. The match erupted in the 73rd minute with both packs wading into each other.

Dragon's hooker, Jones, and Munster prop, Horan, were singled out by referee Chris White and sent to the sin bin, and the 14 remaining Dragons had nothing left. But once again the Munster out half and saviour, Ronan O'Gara, stepped up to the play and slotted two crucial penalty goals to give the Irish side the lead. And with minutes to go, a bright and shining Munster star on the rise, in the form of Jerry Flannery, put the game beyond the heart-broken visitors with an 80th minute try.

However, by failing to score four tries and securing the precious bonus point, Munster slipped further away from Sale and that automatic qualifying spot for the quarter-finals. Next on the agenda was a Friday the 13th clash with old French rivals Castres, away from home, in January. And certainly Friday the 13th will hold a host of new omens for the French journeymen who were handed a whipping from a Munster team on a mission, romping to a 9-46 victory.

Scoring an amazing seven tries and finally getting that precious bonus point, Munster had given themselves a slim lifeline towards making it to the quarter-finals and even getting a home draw—a miracle was most certainly on the cards. That night, Marcus Horan and Shaun Payne both crossed early in the first half before the visitors conceded sloppy tries late in the first 40 minutes.

But man-mountain Paul O'Connell, who was producing the sort of performances that made Martin Johnson look like a tame lamb, and second string scrum half Tomas O'Leary, scored two each in the second half. King of consistency, winger John Kelly, also went over to help Munster record a comfortable victory, and an all-important bonus point ahead of the crunch clash with group leaders Sale.

Marticorena started the ball rolling with a penalty before Ronan O'Gara also scored, as Munster dominated the early stages, culminating in Horan's try after 32 minutes. Payne soon followed that up with another cross over to capitalise on expert team play by the Irish side. Marticorena would not be denied though, and kicked two more penalties to peg back Munster and give struggling Castres a foundation upon which they failed to really build.

Munster responded with brute force, pace and some unexpected nifty back play after the break, and Kelly quickly went over to take advantage of another of O'Gara's deft probing kicks. O'Connell soon followed that up with his first of the match and wasted little time adding a second, having secured the bonus.

With Castres completely disillusioned and in disarray, O'Gara once again proved the fulcrum of the rampant visitors and set up O'Leary with some alert play close to the line, before the latter bagged his second score to finish an incredible evening's rugby for Munster.

With two home wins followed by two away victories to Castres and the Gwent Dragons, Munster were all but out of the Heineken Cup—but the emphatic victory away to Castres had sent an SOS out to the Thomond faithful. A call that was duly answered with style.

As we've seen from players, pundits and fans alike, few people in Ireland, let alone Limerick or Cork, would say that Munster are not a force to be reckoned with at Thomond Park, and miracles are not unknown around those parts. Gloucester and Saracens would be the first to agree. But when the Sharks were due to arrive for the final pool match on 21 January 2006, Munster were practically dead and buried.

Munster needed to topple Sale but needed to score a bonus point in the process, something that had not been done against a Sale side that were going from strength to strength since beating Munster in October. For many it was simply a case of Sale turning up and knocking the Irish team out of the park.

What was putting double pressure on Munster was the prospect that Leinster looked certain to qualify from their pool, and the thought that they would go through while Munster were knocked out was too terrible a thought for the Munster faithful. It may have been a tiny factor that influenced the unbelievable events that unfolded that night in Limerick.

Once again Munster did the impossible, with an 82nd minute try that would clinch the bonus point and enabled them to leapfrog Sale Sharks at the top of Pool 1. This would be Munster's 24th successive victory at Thomond Park, and by reversing their defeat at Sale in the opening round, they became only the second team in Heineken Cup history to register 50 victories.

However, that night will only be remembered for one thing; an atmosphere that would have sent Goliath himself scampering from the spirit and voice of the Munster crowd, shoulder to shoulder in solidarity, willing their charges onto an unbelievable win. Before the first whistle, when the Sale team ran out onto the pitch, they must have felt that 80 minutes later they would be looking forward to a comfortable home quarter-final against one of the lesser French teams. Moments later, when the Munster team emerged from the bowels of Thomond, a roar that would have woken the dead may have changed their perspective.

It seemed at times that the stands began to shake under the weight of expectation as the capacity crowd amalgamated to one voice that would lift an already inspired team to the status of giants. A repeat of the opener was never on the cards.

As expected, the game got off to a ferocious start and French referee Joel Jutge issued the first of three yellow cards for fighting to Sale's Argentinean lock Ignacio Fernandez Lobbe, after only four minutes. Ronan O'Gara opened the scoring with a sixth minute penalty, which his outside half rival Charlie Hodgeson matched five minutes later.

The tempo was being ruled by the beating hearts and chants of the 16th, 17th, and 18th extra man being provided by the frenzied supporters. Sure enough, just before Lobbe returned, Munster struck the first blow when they drove inspirational skipper Anthony Foley over for yet another try. As the stadium erupted, the Sale players looked on in disbelief at the position they were in.

Like a metronome, O'Gara added the conversion, and did the same on the half hour when Ian Dowling dived in at the left corner—suddenly miracle number three was on the cards, and Sale were visibly rocked.

Now Munster really were on a roll, and two minutes after Sale's England lock Chris Jones and Munster's Irish international prop Marcus Horan had hand-bagged their way into the sin bin, a new hero was born into the Limerick hall of fame, as talented youngster Barry Murphy snatched try number three, sprinting over 50 metres to touch down.

O'Gara converted to stretch the lead to 18 points, and the only consolation for Sale was a third Hodgeson penalty on the stroke of half-time. 40 minutes were left in the game, and all Munster needed to do was shut Sale down and secure that final try to clinch what would ultimately be one of their greatest victories and resurrections ever.

But Sale have not gotten where they are today by lying down when the going gets rough, and sure enough Munster were unable to maintain their momentum in the second half as they went in search of the fourth try. Sale tightened up their scrum and lineout and once again began to probe and test Munster's line of defence, reverting to that bully boy tactic that had served them so well in the opening game.

Once again the crowd was on hand, like a teacher patrolling the school yard, howling, screaming and punishing any of the Sale player's misconduct. As time ticked away it looked like Munster had blown it, and while they would win the game, without the bonus they were effectively out of the competition. Time and time again they tried to once again break through the visitor's defence, only to be repelled.

Had Munster used up their quota of miracles? Not a chance. As all Munster fans now know, good things come to those who wait, and the 13,000 Munster faithful, fingernails chewed down to their knuckles, watched on as the stadium clock ticked on past 80 minutes. Two minutes later, the dream became a reality when stalwart flanker and Munster legend, David Wallace, rounded off a flowing move, with forwards and backs combining effortlessly, to cross the line and snatch the try that would seal Sale's fate.

O'Gara added the conversion and Munster were on their way to the quarter-finals as pool winners. The noise around Thomond Park was deafening as, once again, an act of God highlighted a sense of pride, heroism and community that saw Munster march on towards that holiest of Grails, the Heineken Cup.

By now the men in Leinster had also qualified for the quarter-finals, only to be drawn against tournament favourites Toulouse in the heart of French rugby, away from their Donnybrook home. Both games would be played on the same day. Increased demand, however, saw Munster ousted from their comfortable hunting ground at Thomond Park, sent instead to the Dublin 4 ground of Lansdowne Road.

The Sale game had vaulted Munster to second favourites for the competition behind Toulouse, who with ex-Leinster man Trevor Brennan, were looking forward to putting both Irish teams out of the competition. Leinster had learned from the example set by the men from the south of Ireland, and had mustered a travelling support to be reckoned with, invading Toulouse with a sea of blue and gold, dreaming once again that an Irish team could pull it out of the bag.

Back in Dublin, Munster faced the might of the weakest French side to qualify in the form of Perpignan. Both quarter-finals would take place on 1 April, but Leinster would be playing earlier in the day.

Despite the increased capacity in Lansdowne Road, tickets were once again thin on the ground, and almost 60,000 people had turned up to watch the game in a 40,000 capacity stadium. The scramble was on, and e-bay proved the new buy and sell for rugby touts, who were flogging pairs of terrace tickets for €500.

On the morning of the games, the whole of the country was gripped with rugby fever, and for the first time in over two weeks, every Dublin 4 pub was thronged with Munster fans, desperate for a glimpse of Leinster's fate against the Toulouse machine. That afternoon, in the bright sun, in the French capital of rugby, Leinster sprang one of the greatest shocks in the tournament's history, with a 41-35 triumph at Le Stadium.

The Lion's pulled off an incredible victory before 37,000 people, dethroning the reigning and three-time Heineken European Cup kingpins in spectacular fashion. It was a stunning result with the score line failing to reflect their dominance, and Contepomi was the pick of the team, courtesy of a magnificently composed display in the Number 10 jersey.

Meanwhile, Munster guaranteed Ireland's part in this year's Heineken Cup final with a workmanlike 19-10 victory over Perpignan at Lansdowne Road. Yet many Munster fans had woken up on Saturday morning hearing stories that Ronan O'Gara was a doubtful starter after tweaking a hamstring on Thursday. Many at a packed Lansdowne Road thought it was an April Fool's joke, but all such worries were set aside when O'Gara ran onto the field before kick-off and proceeded to give another assured, match-winning performance.

The Cork man scored 14 points in a tough, dogged quarter-final that was a million miles away from the champagne rugby in Toulouse a few hours earlier. With what can really be described as the classic example of ten-man rugby, the Munster forwards literally pummelled the Perpignan pack to pieces in one of the most physical displays in the Cup competition. The weather perhaps highlighted the difference in styles that Saturday, as Munster enjoyed the damp blustery conditions of Ireland in the spring, preventing the visitors from unleashing a successful back line assault while they kept things tight.

Munster had come closest to breaking the deadlock in a cagey opening quarter when O'Connell spilled the ball as he crossed the line following Donnacha O'Callaghan's break. But after Perpignan prop Nicolas Mas was sent to the sin bin for illegally slowing a Munster attack, the giant Ireland lock went one better to grab the opening score. The lineout giant and all round pillar of strength set up a scoring position for Munster yards from the try line and was on hand to crash over on 21 minutes after Perpignan had repelled a series of drives. O'Gara converted for a 7-0 home lead and all looked rosy for Munster.

However Perpignan, who made their only Heineken Cup final appearance at this venue in 2003, showed they were not about to roll over in front of a handful of their own supporters. Perhaps the pressure of knowing they had the chance of a mouth-watering semi-final against their Dublin 4 rivals were playing on Munster minds, and an edgy atmosphere penetrated the usually vibrant supporters in Lansdowne that day. This alien atmosphere appeared to permeate onto the playing surface, and the away team capitalised on Munster's seemingly endless string of nervous errors.

France centre David Marty seized on a loose ball in midfield, and suddenly Mathieu Bourret had a clear path to the corner. They were back in the game. The young wing converted expertly from the touchline on 31 minutes and added a penalty to leave Perpignan ahead at the break and Munster facing more Lansdowne Road heartbreak.

But both the fans and team had come too far together to allow Leinster outshine them in their own competition, and the second half ushered a different, more physical performance. Something special had been brewing between 9 and 10 for Munster all season, and O'Gara was about to unleash a vein of form that had been threatened since he first graced the red of Munster. The inspired fly half got Munster back in front with two penalties in five minutes straight after the break to steal a 13-10 lead.

It was make or break time for Perpignan as they pressed hard, only to be repelled again by a now impenetrable red line of defence. Something had to give as the French began to get frustrated by the waves of Munster attacks and defensive plays. Bourret missed two crucial kicks in the second half as Perpignan's indiscipline, born of frustration, cost them two yellow cards, and Julien Laharrague missed two speculative drop goal attempts, allowing the red army to take control of the game and strangle the life out of any signs of a French victory. In truth that was the end of it as far as the visitors chances of winning were concerned.

O'Gara ruled the roost, giving an educated display in the Number 10 shirt, keeping his cool to slot over two more penalties and ease Munster through to a thrilling semi-final date against Leinster. As fans filtered out of the grey backdrop of Lansdowne, the clouds split and the sun peaked through. It was a far cry from the electric back line display that Leinster delivered in Toulouse, but it was a win nonetheless.

The end result was Ireland 2, France 0, and a mouth- watering semi-final was set up for Lansdowne Road, with both teams doing battle on Sunday, 23 April. This also churned out a different battle off the pitch as both batches of supporters vied to outdo their opponents in the national team's home ground, which in turn led to an intense scramble for tickets, and as happened in the past, when supply exceeds demand, it is the Munster fans that were willing to pay for the privilege of supporting their beloved team.

Despite both teams getting an equal allocation of 20,000 tickets each, Lansdowne Road was awash with a sea of red and white as the Leinster fans were corralled into the North Terrace. The result was that for the first time ever, the Munster team had managed to transfer the Thomond factor to Lansdowne Road, and opened up the possibility that they might even be able to exorcise the ghost of the Wasps debacle two years before.

Home support aside, there never appears to be a close game between both provinces, with one team usually seizing the initiative early on and demolishing the other. Such was the case during their first meeting, back in October in Musgrave Park, when a win moved Munster back to the top of the Celtic League table, after they ran in five tries in a one-sided game.

Marcus Horan, Mick O'Driscoll, Denis Leamy, John Kelly and Ronan O'Gara touched down for Munster that day, despite the fact that Leinster's Felipe Contepomi, playing at inside centre, had kicked the Dublin side to a 5-9 half time lead. The rout left Leinster with the dubious record of not having won in Munster since an 18-24 victory at Dooradoyle in 1998. But Leinster were soon to have revenge. On New Year's Eve, a Celtic League record crowd of 14,000 turned out at the RDS to watch the home side turn over Munster 35-23.

With Contepomi in his more destructive position of out half, Leinster touched down four times, the Argentinean running the show with aplomb. His tally of two tries, three conversions and three penalties, and a try each from Shane Horgan and hooker Brian Blaney, ensured Leinster went into the semi-final as favourites.

That sunny Sunday morning, the team sheets showed that Munster showcased most of Ireland's pack while in Brian O'Driscoll, Gordon D'Arcy and Shane Horgan, Leinster possessed the Test team's most dangerous strike runners.

And naturally both quarter-final victories and the different styles of play that pulled both sides through allowed various pundits to bill the titanic confrontation as the struggle between brain and brawn or style versus substance. It was the blue blooded boys from the Pale against the red-blooded mountain from the South.

This game was being pitched as the nearest thing rugby will ever get to the atmosphere of an All-Ireland final, and could easily have filled the halls of Croke Park. In terms of passion and colour, the pundits were right, and in this humble observer's opinion, was where the battle was won and lost. It may be a bitter pill to swallow for the Leinster men but that question was answered before one ball had been passed, goal had been kicked, or lineout won.

When the Munster men ran out of that tunnel, the roar that erupted from the apparent 3 to 1 difference in fan backing more than silenced the 'home supporters'. The writing was on the wall for BO'D and his charges, and it simply read 'The end is nigh'. It was Census Day in the Republic of Ireland, and by the look of Lansdowne Road that Sunday, the history books will record that Munster was depopulated.

Maybe the over population of Leinster will mean an influx in Government spending for the eastern province, as the population nearly doubled—and for now they had taken up residence in the East and West Stands, and on top of the East and South terraces. Europe, after all, has become Munster's greatest stage, the Heineken Cup their greatest tragedy. Until now. This was their sixth semi-final appearance since 2000, and they were not going to blow it.

Munster went straight on to the attack from the kick-off, and O'Gara opened the scoring with a penalty goal in only the second minute. A Paul O'Connell steal at a Leinster lineout set up a royal try-scoring opportunity, and back rower Denis Leamy was shoved over the line to extend his side's lead. The visitors lost centre John Kelly to a shoulder injury after 15 minutes, and Leinster gradually got back into the game. Fly-half Felipe Contepomi kicked a penalty goal from in front, but the good work was undone when O'Connell was taken out at a lineout and O'Gara converted the penalty.

A controversial decision to penalise Contepomi gave O'Gara the chance to slot his fourth goal of the match, and Contepomi's poor game got considerably worse when he dragged a simple shot at goal well wide. In truth the Leinster fly-half, poor Felipe, had a nightmare with his kicking out of hand, even fluffing one of four restarts in the first half, but he was also poor about the park.

What may have had a lot to do with it was the constant attention lavished on him by the towering back rower, Denis Leamy. Through his undeterred presence he ensured that Contepomi was not allowed the time or space to produce a similar performance to the match winning game he played in Toulouse two weeks previously. And in all truth and fairness, he was merely the most prominent player to fold in front of the Munster bandwagon.

There were some brave counter-attacks by the backs outside him, but it was always from too deep. Every time Leinster created a promising opening they would either spill the ball, pass it carelessly, knock it on, turn it over, or give away a needless penalty. Still, the stifling of the Argentinean was a particular crowd pleaser and along with the seemingly endless renditions of 'The Fields of Athenry' began a ritual taunting of the Number 10 as his tally of errors increased. Munster took a 16-3 lead into the final exchanges of the first half, and that remained the score as a late O'Gara attempt sneaked past the wrong side of the upright.

Contepomi had the first chance to open the second-half scoring, but kicking into the rather tame Leinster supporters didn't improve his fortune much as his angled attempt hit a post. It summed up Leinster's afternoon as their opponents dominated territory and possession in the third quarter. Munster however, did not have it all their own way as the gaping hole that was Munster's second centre opened up and swallowed yet another potential partner for Halstead with a freak injury.

Incredibly, with only 15 minutes left on the clock, Kelly's replacement, Rob Henderson, limped off and Contepomi managed to narrow the margin to a measly 10 points with a point-blank penalty goal. Munster's Pucciarello was sin binned for repeated infringements, but once again Contepomi's kick was wide and they were again let off the hook.

In what could be described as the Ronan O'Gara show, the Cork man put paid to any thoughts of a Leinster comeback with a virtuoso try, grounding the ball with vim in front of the thousands of ecstatic fans in the South Terrace. His conversion may have sealed a famous victory, but Munster weren't finished putting the boot in just yet. The final nail in Leinster's coffin came when South African centre Trevor Halstead intercepted a Leinster attack and ran 70 metres for the final try of the game.

Once again Munster would stride the centre stage at the Millennium Stadium in Cardiff, but for the first time it was to the detriment of fellow Irishmen. The Leinster Lions skipper, Brian O'Driscoll, was more than a little philosophical when commenting on the Munster victory.

'The score line very much flatters them. They were in a far tougher game than it suggests.'

And he may have been right. If Dennis Hickey had managed to finish off one of his mazy runs, or Contepomi had gotten out of the other side of the bed, who knows what would have happened? But for Munster, destiny had come a-knocking, and they had answered the call.

After the game, Munster captain Anthony Foley reiterated how much winning had meant to his team:

'Reaching the final is what we set out to do at the start of the season. It's one of those things you believe you can do, so it's nice to achieve it,' he said. 'Now we're there, we'd like to give a good account of ourselves. We have a good chance of winning it—it's 50-50—as there are only two teams left. We played Biarritz last year so we know a great deal about them, especially as their personnel hasn't changed too much. But that's for another week.'

Another week, a third Heineken Cup final, and against more French opposition in the form of Biarritz. Third time would finally be a charm, and Munster would eventually lift that most coveted of trophies; the Heineken Cup.

MUNSTER RUGBY FACT:

"The Claw" Has a Saving Grace

When the final whistle blew in the Millennium stadium, injured players, subs and former players came streaming on to the pitch. As Peter Clohessy made his way forward, he was confronted by a steward who insisted that his pass did not allow him pitch-side access. Lucky for 'The Claw', and luckier still for the steward, Sky Sports pundit Dewi Morris slipped his Sky pass to Clohessy, allowing him to celebrate with his former team mates.

'We've achieved something special and we realise the effect it has on people's lives, whether they live in Munster or abroad.'
– Man of the Match Peter Stringer after winning the Heineken Cup

Chapter 12: The wait is over and history is made — Munster are Champions of Europe

Saturday, 20 May is a date that will have a major significance in the lives of thousands of Irish rugby fans for ever more. An act of God was unleashed upon the sporting world, as one of the greatest achievements in Irish sport occurred: Munster were hailed as kings of Europe.

In the past the best thing that I could say about 20 May was that both Cher and Jimmy Stewart were born that day—thank God, something has changed that forever. And the context of the victory and its dramatic significance for Irish sport in general cannot be over-weighed.

Given the indigenous nature of GAA and the lack of international competition, there will never be a European Championship of note in which to achieve ultimate domination. Likewise in soccer, where the lack of funding and the sheer professionalism of the Premiership clubs across the water leave the possibility of a League of Ireland team lifting either the UEFA or Champion's League trophy aloft a virtual impossibility. The same can be said for cricket, tennis, swimming and most of the other sports played in this country.

So for a remarkable side to defeat the professional teams throughout Europe, to lift the crown of European champions has not only afforded Munster the respect and glory they richly deserve, but has also placed the province and country on a world stage for other nations to stare at with envy. It is a feat and achievement that is a rare occurrence in Irish sporting history, where so often the mantra of gallant loser—heroic failure—has been enough to gain sympathy votes from around the world.

At 5.01pm in the Millennium Stadium, a country joined in the swirling voluminous support of the marauding Red Army, as Captain Anthony Foley lifted the Holy Grail of European Rugby, The Heineken Cup trophy aloft, completing the most epic journey since Ulysses himself was blown off course. Not only did they do it the hard way, they had also at last thrown off the shadow of an Ulster side that had pinched the title in a year where both English and Welsh teams had boycotted the competition, outdoing that achievement into the process.

But the joyous scenes that pulsated around the swinging dome and the thousands of Munster fans encased within was a far cry from hours earlier, when tension and fear were part and parcel of the festivities. That morning in Cardiff, the sun broke and thousands of hopeful and hung-over Munster fans crept from whatever dark place they had spent the night, biting nails or whatever they could find to stave off the anxious feelings that threatened to consume them as their heroes attempted to make it third time lucky. The dreaded thought of failure allowed for an insanely charged atmosphere to radiate around the Welsh city, as fans debated the end result with pride and vigour.

Back home in Limerick something similar was happening, as thousands assembled on the streets in front of massive screens to cheer on the Munster men. Little did they know that this mass protest against failure would provide Munster with the hammer to finally put the nail into the Biarritz coffin and leave the Millennium Stadium with the Heineken Cup.

Everywhere you went in the city or province that day there were banners hoisted in support of the players and management, and once again the tales and legends of the great New Zealand victory were being dusted off the shelves and passed down to anyone who would listen. As the weight of expectation from fans both at home and abroad reached critical mass, the Munster squad were deposited into the Millennium Stadium's dome with the roof closed for what would be the most important game of their careers.

Thousands of fans had spent millions of Euro on making the final and ensuring the Welsh GNP doubled, allowing the publicans to build another story on their already lavish country homes. While the French bitched and moaned about the dispersment of tickets that allowed Kidney and company the use of the Red Army with their WMD, the team were in danger of weaving the rope that would eventually become long enough to hang themselves. A loss that day may have proved the straw that would break the camels back, and end the Munster dream.

By now, everybody knows what happened that afternoon in Paris, every vital move and every pulsating moment, but it is something all sports fans relish every time they recall the agony and the ecstasy of it all. It was a day to savour, but from the start, it didn't look that way.

Minutes after the opening kick off, the almost inevitable happened, and once again Munster were back against the wall, screwed from an inattentive lines man who allowed Sereli Bobo the luxury of stepping on the whitewash before grounding the ball, gifting Biarritz and their paltry contingent of supporters a 7-0 lead. Munster were going to have to do it the hard way again.

But staring into the abyss of 2000 and the one that got away, that *Je ne sais quoi* that has gotten them out of so many tight scrapes finally kick started and they took the game by the scruff of the neck, wading into the French team who were being driven by the exceptional Dimitri Yachvili. Munster turned things around. Munster seemed to absorb the cruel punishment of the try, (perhaps remembering the outlandish decision of Steve Landers refusing to acknowledge John O'Neill's try against Stade Français in the Lille semi-final in 2001) set to their task despite the shock and began to batter the French visitors.

Seven minutes into the game, the referee's arm went out signalling, that the men in red had a penalty, but O'Gara decided on a cross field kick—an adventurous but risky move—and to everyone's dismay it was picked off by Bobo. Luckily, the play was called back for an earlier offence and O'Gara decided to have a shot at goal.

Surely with the horrific memories of the Northampton final in his head, the first kick would be all important for confidence and composure Bang! It dissected the posts, Munster were on the board, and the Number 10 began to take control of a game he would run for the rest of the day. Then as the Munster pack, and in particular the back-row, began to bombard the Biarritz line, Munster gained another penalty in the Biarritz half, but again elected to go for touch instead of the posts.

While many of the commentators and pundits were screaming at the players, the fans realised the signalling of intent and 'The Field's of Athenry' began to echo from the rafters of the magnificent ground. They were going for it.

Two similar penalties and four minutes later Munster were back attacking the Biarritz line. After battering the blind side they spread it wide to O'Gara, whose clever chip was flicked up by Anthony Horgan, who sent Paul O'Connell driving into the Basque defence. Munster then battered the blindside for a few minutes before O'Gara offloaded to the marauding figure of South African centre Trevor Halstead. As he crashed over the line Munster went in front and it appeared for the time being that they were in complete control, with one clear hand on the trophy.

O'Gara added a touchline conversion, and they led by three points. It was back to business. Irish prop Marcus Horan was unfairly adjudged to have collapsed the scrum and the nifty Biarritz Number Nine slotted a 21 yard penalty to briefly take the lead, the last time they would be in front for the rest of the match.

Perhaps what the referee hadn't noticed was the pressure that was being directed on loose-head Marcus Horan, who made a miraculous recovery and was in fact lucky to be on the pitch after an astounding battle.

It was clear from that scrum that Horan was a target, and it's a credit to the prop that this was the only time the scrum creaked under Biarritz pressure. In an *Irish Times* interview with John O'Sullivan after the match, he revealed the painful road to making the team and finally winning the title.

'I knew it was going to be tight if I was going to make the final, but I had a goal and stuck to it. To be honest, last Friday week, I felt a twinge in training and thought I had done something bad again. But it was a case of just stretching the muscle and it eased out.

'The first scrum was always going to be the litmus test. It was such a relief. I think there was a little euphoria there as it removed any lingering doubt, even if it was only 1%. I was cocky enough to scrummage off my bad leg at one stage. It was tough out there, physically very hard, but we just kept working away, picking and driving and making them tackle again and again. Both teams earned the yards they got.

'When I came off, I didn't know what to do with myself. I felt powerless and when Freddie (Pucciariello) went down injured I had to be restrained from running back on.'

Horan said in the same interview that he was delighted to be joined on the pitch by players who had been ruled out by injury, such as Barry Murphy, Christian Cullen, Frankie Sheehan and Frankie Roche. 'We're a squad and what we achieve we achieve together. Everyone contributed.'

In the heat of the battle, Horan stood tall and stuck to his task from that scrum on. For the rest of the first half every Biarritz attack was met by the unmovable line of defence of the Munster team as Foley, Leamy and Wallace bounced the French stars back like rucking pads.

As Munster attacked in return, forcing a penalty, O'Gara once again opted to kick for the corner instead of taking a shot at the posts, and Munster laid siege to the Biarritz line. Time and again they swarmed near the Biarritz line, but they were desperately repelled, just inches from glory. It looked like the French might have gotten away with their lead intact as half-time approached. That was until a moment of brilliance turned the game on its head.

31 minutes into the game, wiley scrum half Peter Stringer showed why he is the number one scrum half in the country (and why video analysis is probably one of the most vital developments in professional rugby) and provided the Munster team and their following with a try that will be remembered by the little man and everybody else for years to come.

It had been noted by analysts that when defending a scrum close to their line, the usually savvy Basque men tended to allow their blindside wing to be drawn infield.

And as the fates aligned the rugby planets together, Munster were awarded a five metre scrum, allowing them to deploy a tactical American football-type play. Before Stringer fed the scrum, Anthony Horgan left his station on the right wing, and like a line backer, fed the bait to his marker Sereli Bobo, hoping he would follow him across. Like a lamb to the slaughter, the Fijian took the bait and Stringer could see him shift away from the touchline out of the corner of his eye. From that point it was game on.

Feverishly quick the Corkman dipped in underneath the protection of Leamy at Number Eight and managed to feign a long dive pass left, out to O'Gara. Instead, he changed tack and direction, bursting right and over the line before blindside Serge Betson realised what had happened. After 11 years and 80 European ties, Stringer had finally nailed the critics of his lack of breaking ability with this wonderful move and started the Munster ball rolling in this cliff-hanger of a final.

In a post match interview to the world's media, he revealed how the move had come about. 'I saw their wing creeping away from the touchline and I'd been keeping an eye out for that. It had been written down from the analysis we'd done on them as something that might come in useful. I had a look before picking the ball up and I had a hunch that he (Bobo) had drifted inside. It was always going to be worth a shot. I just had to run a few metres and you could say I was very glad to find there was nobody standing in my way.

'It's hard to say what Munster's secret is. It is something that comes from where we live, it's a special place to be. You meet your friends in the street, and you see how much games like this mean to them.'

This was a feeling shared by all the players and fans alike, and after the try, Munster's dominance was beginning to tell all over the park. In the lineout, pressure at two and four forced hooker Benoit August to throw to six but he overcooked the pass and it landed for Wallace to run onto it, making more inroads into the Biarritz half.

Biarritz's lifeline came in the form of the half time whistle and both teams retired to their dressing rooms underneath the stands. Incredibly the organisers had clearly prepared for the Munster army and adopted the half time entertainment accordingly. While it was no Superbowl extravaganza, it was not without its Janet Jackson moment, as rather than the usual 'Kick for Charity' Heineken competition, the fans were treated to a live rendition of 'Stand Up and Fight', Thomond Park's home anthem.

The French must have been wondering what they had done to the Welsh in the past and secretly decided that Kerrygold would no longer be the butter of choice, as Munster fans threatened to raise the roof with their songs and cheers, but attention turned to business when suddenly both teams were back on the paddock.

Starting like they finished the first half, Munster were back on the attack, and a series of up and unders led to Biarritz straying offside, leaving O'Gara and his new game plan to slot the 21 metre penalty—20-10 to the men in red.

Biarritz began to step up the tempo and looked like they might have pulled something out of the bag, with international Damien Traille making a mazy run, only to be scragged by John Hayes before Leamy thundered in to force the turnover. But on 47 minutes a loose lineout tap back forced John Hayes to play the ball in an offside position and Dead Eye Dimitri, Yachvili, put the three points on the board.

Three minutes later, Leamy was adjudged to have made a high tackle on Imanol Harinordoquy, who appeared to have World Cup fever, diving and rolling all over the ground from a reasonably innocuous challenge. One Yachvili kick later and suddenly Munster were only four points ahead. Nerves were fraying.

At 55 minutes, Donnacha O'Callaghan stole a Biarritz lineout and the Munster pack mauled towards the opposing 22, only to turn over the ball to some dubious rucking. This led to an outbreak of anger and emotion as both teams lashed out with their respective handbags, forcing a break in play and leaving the crowd needing oxygen and some stiffer drinks.

Then as if the game needed any more talking points, the crunch turning point arrived and effectively ended Biarritz's challenge in the Heineken Cup final. With 60.46 on the clock, four points in the difference, and Munster beginning to sway in the breeze with seemingly relentless waves of attack from the Frenchmen, a blessed break in play came in the form of a player receiving attention from medical staff.

With the tanks empty and the players sucking in precious oxygen, channel hopping began on the big screens and suddenly the scenes of hordes of Munster supporters filling O'Connell Street in Limerick flashed on the screens in the stadium.

As a Mexican sound wave created a sonic boom of support, the players began to search the stands for the source of the resurgence, and they too noticed the incredible scenes before their eyes. Whatever rugby gods were shining down on Munster that day, or whatever Rupert Murdoch-based wizardry was in force, there were no pictures of the 20 Biarritz fans watching the game in their local café to balance out the top-heavy equation. Even if there had been 20,000 French fans hoisting flags under the Eiffel tower it would have mattered not, as the damage had been done. The Munster players discovered energy and muscles that had never existed before and rebooted the team and their efforts. They were never going to lose it after that.

Speaking to the world's media after the game, inspirational hooker Jerry Flannery remembered the huddle and exactly what had happened.

'We were flat out and were all sucking serious diesel at that stage. Then Paul O'Connell tapped me and pointed up at the screen just as all the fans had started going crazy. Oh my God, it was Limerick, with all those people in the shot, and suddenly everybody knew and remembered why we were here. I suddenly felt energised all over again.

'This win isn't so much about 15 players, it's about who we are, where we live, the people we know and the people who, even though I may never have met them, know me. It just seems when it comes to Munster Rugby and this team, everybody is a stakeholder.'

And that was it, game over, as more than a second, more like an eight wind carried Munster over the last 20 minutes, and they squeezed the life out of Biarritz. To give them their due, Biarritz wanted this too much to let it go quietly and continued to make it one hell of a game. The last seven or eight minutes were excruciating, as Munster foiled repeated French sorties into their half, denying them the vital try.

Two new onlookers in the form of the substituted Paul O'Connell and Marcus Horan looked close to mental breakdown as they counted the clock down, now powerless as to the outcome of the game. Then suddenly the ball was in touch, the final whistle blown, and the game was over—Munster were the 2006 Heineken Cup champions. The intense emotion was unquenchable as towering giants broke down with towering giants, at the fore of the world's stage.

The crowd exploded in a cacophony of whoops, cheers, songs, and one gigantic sigh of relief, and it was almost as if the roof of the stadium had opened to allow a great cloud of pressure escape the tension, morphed into excitement. The atmosphere changed completely. The wait was over, the journey complete. Red flares burned, songs were sung and the team began their lap of honour.

Then, all too quickly the team were ushered together, and as television time dictated, the presentation was done to facilitate potential advertisement slots. Drenched by a unique bottle of Heineken Champagne, the man they call Axel, came forward to lift the Heineken Cup trophy. After the game, the celebrations began all over Cardiff, Limerick, Munster and Ireland, the streets erupting with joy as the players struggled to come to terms with the magnitude of their victory. The bridesmaids had finally managed a proposal and wedding of their own, but in true Munster fashion were as gracious in victory as they had been in defeat.

One man who has epitomised the valour and spirit of the Munster effort is second row Lion Donnacha O'Callaghan. Often forgotten beside his titanic second row partner, O'Callaghan shone in the final game and is as deserving of praise as any. He played out of his skin, was battered and bruised, but when the final whistle blew, all the pain was forgotten instantly.

'It wasn't the prettiest of finals; they normally aren't. We'll just look at parts of it and wonder how we managed to hold them out. But to be honest, I couldn't care less,' he told the media.

'We said all week that we wanted to perform, we wanted to go well. That was the thing we learnt from the last two (finals). You have to go and win finals. We did that to a degree. We scored two tries. Strings's was a beauty, a fine individual effort. That's what you need, fellas, stepping up on big occasions and getting scores for you.

'We pride ourselves on a bit of honesty. We like to take teams head on. It was really tough. The lineout was a huge game within the game. They have a very good defence. We were just delighted to get our fair share of ball.'

Describing the achievement in itself was more difficult.

'It's hard to put into words ... so proud of the fellas around you. Whatever about yourself you see the amount of hard work they put in. Just to wake up and be European champions. We've woken up a few times and it's been a rotten old feeling. I can't wait for tomorrow morning.'

He's loathe to draw comparison with the Triple Crown win. 'They're both hugely special. It's a great honour to play for your country. We've brought something in here where the jersey means an awful lot to us. You just want to pass it on to the next guy with the same respect it was given to you. It's hard to compare. Fellas were just as pleased when we won a Triple Crown. It's great for the supporters.'

But it was clear the next day that arrogance wasn't a word in the vocabulary of these players, as the threat of merely fading away into the mediocrity of European rugby loomed ahead. The eventual victory had left the champions with a new problem, and nobody relishes the tag of one hit wonders, a prospect one giant was unwilling to accept. The next day, as people thronged to the streets to see their idols and the trophy's return, Munster's talismanic hero, Paul O'Connell was unwilling to rest on the laurels of the recent victory.

Like every consummate professional, he now has the taste of victory and wants it all, but he is wary of success and the possibility of eyes falling off the prize after finally getting their hands on the Heineken Cup.

'Our Celtic League form this season has been poor, and we need to start performing better than that,' said the Ireland and Lions lock when speaking to reporters in Limerick. 'If you look at teams like Wasps and Leicester, when they were winning the Heineken Cup they were also dominating their domestic league. We've had a few hard years in this tournament, and I hope people appreciate we weren't showboating afterwards," he added, reflecting on the unforgettable scenes of celebration as the Munster players shared their triumph with 70,000 ecstatic supporters at the Millennium Stadium.

'We wanted to enjoy the occasion after what had been a lot of heartache pursuing this competition.'

While they may have enjoyed the competition as players, watching the journey has become a full-time past time for many of the loyal fans from all corners of the country. While it is clear that the first one is the all important one, and this crop of players has just joined the ranks of the '78 brigade, there is a part of Munster that is sad the journey is over. While the players will tell you that a great monkey is off their backs, the romance of the chase was what kept the fans' fires stoked and burning.

Now all we are left with is the start of a new journey, the road to the retention of that title.

But one thing is for sure; one key element that has allowed the Munster team to lift that trophy is the existence of the X-factor, the phenomenon that helped them through the tight scrapes. Be it the crowd, the ground, the songs, the history or the traditions; all combined will now have to adjust as a new journey lies ahead. The only question now is whether Munster will settle for having achieved their hearts' desire, or will they redouble their efforts.

And thankfully even in the ecstatic aftermath, there was already a mood to do it again.

'We have to keep producing if we want to be truly great champions like Wasps or Toulouse,' insists Donnacha O'Callaghan.

The 2007 double is something that is in the hearts and minds of all fans and players and I know I will certainly be there. Will you?

MUNSTER RUGBY FACT:

The Enterprise

One group of eight gentlemen desperate to see the 2006 Heineken Cup final hired a 50 foot boat out of Baltimore in Cork and navigated their way across the Irish Sea. The journey took 16-20 hours on the boat in question. They based themselves in Swansea and despite having no accommodation lined up, made their way to Cardiff by train.

Munster's run to the final

21/10/05 19:30. Sale Sharks 27-13 Munster.
Venue: Edgeley Park, Sale. Attendance: 10,704.

29/10/05 17:15. Munster 42-16 Castres Olympique.
Venue: Thomond Park. Attendance: 13,500

10/12/05 13:00. Dragons 8-24 Munster.
Venue: Rodney Parade. Attendance: 8,323.

17/12/05 17:15. Munster 30-18 Dragons.
Venue: Thomond Park. Attendance: 13,200.

13/1/06 20:40. Castres Olympique 9-46 Munster.
Venue: Stade Pierre-Antoine. Attendance: 9,423.

21/1/06 17:15. Munster 31-9 Sale Sharks.
Venue: Thomond Park. Attendance: 13,200.

1/4/06 17:30. QF Munster 19-10 Perpignan.
Venue: Lansdowne Road. Attendance: 48,500.

23/4/06 15:00. SF Leinster 6-30 Munster.
Venue: Lansdowne Road. Attendance: 47,800.

20/5/06 15:00. Final: Biarritz Olympique 19-23 Munster.
Venue: Millennium Stadium Cardiff. Attendance: 74,534+.

The 2006 Heineken Cup final teams

MUNSTER RUGBY

Coach: Declan Kidney

Shaun Payne 15 full back
Anthony Horgan 14 right wing
John Kelly 13 centre
Trevor Halstead 12 centre
Ian Dowling 11 left wing
Ronan O'Gara 10 out half
Peter Stringer 9 scrum half
Marcus Horan 1 prop
Jerry Flannery 2 hooker
John Hayes 3 prop
Donnacha O'Callaghan 4 lock
Paul O'Connell 5 lock
Denis Leamy 6 flanker
David Wallace 7 flanker
Anthony Foley 8 No. 8

Replacements:
Denis Fogarty 16
Federico Pucciariello 17
Mick O'Driscoll 18
Alan Quinlan 19
Tomas O'Leary 20
Jeremy Manning 21
Rob Henerson 22

BIARRITZ OLYMPIQUE PAYS BASQUE

Coaches: Patrice Lagisquet / Jacques Delmas

Nicolas Brusque 15 full back
Jean-Baptiste Gobelet 14 right wing
Philippe Bidabe 13 centre
Damien Traille 12 centre
Sireli Bobo 11 left wing
Julien Peyrelongue 10 out half
Dimitri Yachvili 9 scrum half
Petru-Vladimir Balan 1 prop
Benoit August 2 hooker
Census Johnston 3 prop
Jerome Thion 4 lock
David Couzinet 5 lock
Serge Betsen 6 flanker
Imanol Harinordoquy 7 flanker
Thomas Lievremont 8 No. 8

Replacements:
Benjamin Noirot 16
Benoit Lecouls 17
Olivier Olibeau 18
Thierry Dusatoir 19
Manuel Carizza 20
Julien Dupuy 21
Federico Martin Arramburu 22

The Munster Dream Team

One of the greatest rewards of being a Munster fan (apart from winning the Heineken Cup!) is the divine right to mull over facts and figures, brooding over the final 15.

It is the agonising bar stool search to define that ultimate squad of players that, on their day, could beat any one, anywhere, by a million points, that keeps us talking long into the night.

It's about arguing it out with your mates in a drunken frenzy because they have picked a donkey from 30 years ago in place of the mercurial Keith Wood.

It is a right of passage afforded to all members of the Red Army, and as an honourary one I have decided to exercise my choice.

For what it is worth, here is my ultimate 15, a subjective selection for world domination.

1. Peter Clohessy

It is a strange thing to be known affectionately as "The Claw", but Peter Clohessy has managed to endear himself to the entire Munster Red Army.

His hard nosed attitude to rugby ensured him a regular spot on the national squad but his first love was always the red of Munster.

Seen weeping after the dramatic final win, "The Claw" is a Munster stalwart and the first name down on any dream team sheet.

Marcus Horan can feel a little hard done by but has plenty of time on his hands to oust the man with the Number One jersey.

2. Keith Wood

There really is only one man who could lay true claim to this title and it is Keith Gordon Wood.

The happy hooker has led from the front in every aspect of his sporting life and his position with Munster was no different.

Some critics say he left the hallowed province to lay claim to the Queen's shilling, but he only had eyes for one team and that was Munster.

He also brought the team to their first Heineken Cup final (one they should have won) against Northampton.

Like Horan, Sheehan and Flannery both have time to fight for their place on the list.

3. Ginger Mc Laughlin

There will be few men in the south of Ireland who would disagree with this choice for the Number Three spot.

The fiery prop terrorised provincial and international scrums with his strength and skill in the tight.

There are few men who managed to go toe to toe with Ginger and leave unscathed.

McLaughlin never had the recognition John Hayes received, as the professional era was a thing of the future back then—but is regarded as the greatest prop ever to emerge from Munster.

4. Paul O'Connell

What is left to say about the towering mountain of man mass that is Paul O'Connell?

It is difficult to believe that at the tender age of 26 he has already become one of the greatest players in the world.

His leadership skills and never say die attitude have made him the new great white hope of Irish rugby.

There are few who will forget his tear stained face after the final, showing the true measure of the colossus—red through and through.

5. Mick Galwey

If you could have any player beside you in the second row it would have to be Mick Galwey.

'Gaillaimh' simply ate, breathed and slept Munster in a career that broke his heart on two occasions.

Lifting the Celtic League trophy will have assuaged some of his loss but nothing will have been sweeter for the Shannon man than finally landing the Heineken Cup.

Fought off tough competition from any number of Munster legends, and if there is one thing they are not short of, it is second rows.

6. Donal Lenihan

Not predominantly a back row specialist, Lenihan simply had to make this team.

Perhaps on the pitch Galwey and Lenihan could rotate and share the burden but no greater servant to the cause will you find.

A decorated Lion with a lifetime of Munster caps, Donal Lenihan served Munster Rugby with a hard nosed passion that is still prevalent today.

As a journalist for *The Examiner* he is their biggest fan and hardest critic but few would have grinned as widely as him when Foley hoisted the European Cup.

7. David Wallace

This is a personal choice made more by the heart than the head.

Wallace for me is the best Number Seven in Ireland at the moment and without doubt Munster's hardest worker.

Over his career he has scored tries when Munster looked dead and buried and even managed to wrestle the national team out of trouble on occasion.

Unlucky to have to compete against another true red, Alan Quinlan, but this man has more than proved his worth time and again.

8. Anthony Foley

The captain who lifted the trophy and managed to break the Munster curse in the Heineken Cup competition.

His reputation speaks for itself, missing only one game in Munster's entire Heineken Cup campaign.

He makes the hard yards whenever possible and responded to being dropped from the national team by winning the Heineken Cup.

His willingness to put in the donkey work will make him a massive loss whenever he chooses to retire.

9. Peter Stringer

The tiny scrum half with the big heart and the selective break is a must have on any such list.

His try in the final gave Munster the edge over a revitalised Biarritz and his service to O'Gara has given him the time to run the show.

He certainly has his critics but you would do well to find an equal for "Strings" in any of the history books.

10. Tony Ward

This was the hardest choice to make but over all I feel that Tony Ward has sneaked it.

The man quite simply oozed class and style and his running game was an alien component to the hard graft, caustic style of Munster Rugby.

His unpredictable finesse confused more teams (and sometimes his own team mates), none more prevalent than the All Blacks in 1978.

The fact that he made the change from soccer to rugby so effortlessly is just another string in his legendary bow.

11. Moss Finn

Without doubt one of the few great strike runners for the men in red.

Finn could conjure a break out of nothing and with his real pace was a threat from just about anywhere.

A seductive side step combined with the gift of incredible gear change made him a terror to defences.

12. Mike Mullins

Munster has never really been celebrated for their wealth of centres, a fact mirrored by the crises over the 2006 campaign.

But the willingness of individuals to rise above their station is another element of the Munster phenomenon that has to be recognised.

One man who epitomises this trait is Mullins, who time and again, pulled it out of the bag when all the chips were down.

Quite possibly the most underrated centre in the history of the province but it is time for him to come out of the shadow.

13. Seamus Dennison

The man responsible for the tackle heard round the world in the famous All Blacks victory so long ago.

Now immortalised through song and play, Seamus Dennison was a hard hitting tackler and elusive runner with a reputation to match any of the greats.

Munster backs tended to take a back seat behind the power of the pack but he was a shining light through the tough games.

Never really got the praise he deserved for his creativity but was one of the all time greats.

14. John Kelly

There is no more deserving player on this list than John Kelly who time and again has surpassed expectation and belief to carry the Munster team to victory.

He is not the quickest or strongest winger in the history of the game but his determination and commitment have stood to him on the biggest occasions.

Like Stringer, he has plenty of critics but has still managed international caps and Celtic League and Heineken Cup winner's medals in their spite.

15. Pat Murray

The forgotten full back of Munster Rugby, Murray was quite simply the man for the high ball.

His Velcro hands made him the perfect guardian for the Munster line, even in the slipperiest of conditions.

His willingness to put his head where others wouldn't put a boot made him a favourite with the crowd.

Replacements:

Moss Keane: a legend and deserving of a full place on the list—just too many exceptional second rows grow in Munster.

John Hayes: "The Bull". What is there to say about him except that he is a legend for country and province. A small lack of technical ability sees him take the bench.

Frankie Sheehan: the unluckiest Munster man in the history of the game suffered a terrible neck injury that cost him his place on the Munster and Irish team. It is, however, his work in the past that secures his spot on the bench.

Ronan O'Gara: An incredibly astute and brave out half who runs the Munster machine with poise and ease. At times he lets the occasion get to him, but this is a minor flaw in a massive portfolio.

Donnacha O'Callaghan: Like Keane, Donnacha is unlucky to be on the bench but there are just too many good locks in Munster Rugby (send some to Connaught if you like).